The Am

BIBLE
Answers
Volume 1

with Doug Batchelor

AMAZING FACTS

Published by
Amazing Facts, Inc.
PO Box 1058
Roseville, CA 95678-8058
1-800-538-7275

Edited by Anthony Lester
Cover Design by Haley Trimmer
Text Layout by Greg Solie – Altamont Graphics

ISBN 1-58019-176-2

Table of Contents

Introduction
.... 5

Section 1
The Nature of the Divine and the Human 7

Section 2
The Nature of Sin and Salvation 22

Section 3
Saturday or Sunday 44

Section 4
Heroes and Villians of the Bible 52

Section 5
Your Church and Your Worship 65

Section 6
Biblical Counsel—A Handbook for Life 85

Section 7
Biblical Principles of Life and Death 104

Section 8
The Word of God 117

Introduction

An Amazing Fact: The name of the pilot program, which aired in April 1995, for *Bible Answers Live* was called *Your Questions, Bible Answers.*

Nearly every Sunday night since October 1, 1995, Amazing Facts *Bible Answers Live* has broadcasted out of Sacramento, California, to a potential audience of millions. This live nationwide call-in radio show has been a blessing to the many thousands who have had their Bible questions answered in a biblical and faith-building way. Even more who might never call have received solid spiritual nourishment, helping them grow in their relationship with Christ.

Ironically, when Pastor Doug Batchelor, president of Amazing Facts, conceived the idea of the program, he was warned that religious call-in shows on Sundays often faired poorly. *Bible Answers Live* has shown to be an astounding exception, and is now heard on more than 160 stations nationwide and around the world in places like Canada, Bermuda, the Virgin Islands, Guam, Tahiti, Costa Rica, Belize, South Africa, New Zealand, Singapore, Switzerland, France, and in other European countries. Furthermore, the live streaming broadcast, available at **www.amazingfacts.org**, has opened up a whole new audience, from those in the United States outside a radio listening area to Internet surfers in Japan. It's no wonder that phone lines light up well before *Bible Answers Live* begins and stay busy for the entire hour.

Although the program may sound like a one-man show, much more happens behind the scenes than most listeners are aware. Pastor Doug Batchelor and co-host Pastor Dick Devitt are supported by a full-time regular staff of radio buyers and producers who work each week before and after the broadcast to ensure the best possible program. In addition, many rotating volunteers—including documenters, call screeners, audio engineers, and Bible researchers—give their time to an evangelistic broadcast that is changing lives for the better.

Over the past nine years, it is estimated that Pastor Doug has fielded more than 6,000 questions from callers. Thus this first volume is just the tip of the iceberg of inquiries from listeners who have asked some of the most challenging and thought-provoking questions about the Bible. We hope that Pastor Doug's answers, here revised and expanded with more Bible verses, will give you fresh insights into God's Holy Word and will inspire you to share those insights and this book with others.

Watch for another collection of Bible answers sometime in the future as the Holy Spirit leads. Until then, thank you for listening and for making *Bible Answers Live* a tremendous success.

The Editor

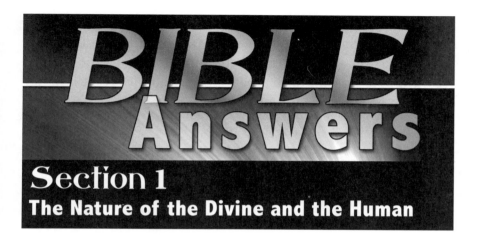

Section 1
The Nature of the Divine and the Human

Who Created God?

 How did God get there if there was nothing there to create Him?

This is a good question, and if I could answer it, I'd probably be God. I can't honestly answer it, but the Bible does say a few words about God's eternal nature. In Psalm 93:2, we are told, "Thy Throne is established of old; thou art from everlasting to everlasting." That means God has always been, and that's difficult for us to understand.

But it remains true—God has always existed. Before time even began, God was there. That's why Jesus refers to Himself as "I Am," meaning He's the self-existing one. He's always been, He always is, and He always will be.

Furthermore, the Bible says, "God is love." You can't love when you're the only person around—not the kind of sacrificing love that God is anyway. So God the Father, Son, and Spirit must have always been, showing love for one another even before the first creature was made.

It's very difficult for humans to imagine because we live in a realm where everything has a beginning and an end. But not so for God—God inhabits eternity (Isaiah 57:15). He can dwell in any and all parts of time at the same time. He lives outside this physical realm, and He created the dimension of time for His creatures. He doesn't have a beginning, and He won't have an end. That is a mystery for all ages.

What Is His Form?

What form does God take? The Bible says He is a spirit, but then man was made in His image.

In John 4:24, we read, "God is a Spirit: And those who worship Him must do so in spirit and truth." But keep in mind that because God is a spirit, it does not mean that He is just ethereal vapor or that He can't have a body. Many believe that spiritual things cannot be physical. That's a misconception. God wants you to be spiritual, and yet you still have a physical body.

Angels are spirits living in a spiritual realm, but the Bible repeatedly identifies them as having a form. "Are they not all ministering spirits sent forth to minister for those who will inherit salvation?" (Hebrews 1:14). God the Father is a spirit, but Daniel sees God on His throne and describes what He looked like in that vision (Daniel 7:9).

Of course, Jesus now has a physical, human body. When He rose from the dead, He received a glorified body. Remember what Jesus said to His disciples: "Behold my hands and my feet, that it is I myself; handle me and see; for a spirit hath not flesh and bones, as ye see me have" (Luke 24:39). He said a spirit, or ghost, does not have flesh like Him. He had a spiritual body, yet He ate in front of them to emphasize that He was real. When we get our new bodies, they will be real but also spiritual—like Jesus now has. "It is sown a natural body; it is raised a spiritual body" (1 Corinthians 15:44). And Philippians 3:21 adds,

"Who shall change our vile body, that it may be fashioned like unto his glorious body." Hebrews 1:3 says, "Who being in the brightness of his glory, and the express image of his person … sat down on the right hand of the Majesty on high." Now, doesn't it ring true that God must have a form if Jesus is sitting at His right hand?

… And What Is His Name?

 My friend says that God commands us to call Him Jehovah? Where does it say that in the Bible?

I'm sure many of our readers have had people come to their doors and have been told that Jehovah is the only appropriate name to call God. There is another group that claims that it must be Yahweh, which is the sacred name of God.

But I respectfully disagree with the idea that God desires we call Him by one name over another. In reality, God goes by many names in the Bible. It is true that God says to Moses in Exodus 6:3, "And I appeared unto Abraham, unto Isaac, and unto Jacob, by the name of God Almighty, but by my name JEHOVAH was I not known to them." However, here God simply revealed a new name to them. And you will find that God continues to reveal new names throughout the Bible. He never says we should use just one name when calling on or referencing Him.

Those who become preoccupied with the idea that we must only address God by one name are, in a certain way, making their God smaller. Indeed, God's names tell us about His character. For instance, He also says we should call him Wonderful, Counselor, the Mighty God, and Everlasting Father.

And Jesus also has many names: He's called Alpha and Omega, the Lamb, the Beginning and the End, the Gate, the Door, and Son of God … so many names it would be impractical to list them all here! The real issue is not by what name we should use when speaking with God, though it should always be done with reverence, holiness, and with a sense of awe.

The real issue is whether or not we honor and exalt His Word. Psalm 138:2 says, "For You have magnified Your word above all Your name." Indeed, each language has different names to refer to God; but the real uniting force is how God's Word transcends language, or simple words, and affects all people regardless of the name one chooses to call Him.

A Jealous God?

Q. The Bible says God is a "jealous God." Wouldn't this mean God is imperfect?

A. If a man loves his wife and knows that she is having an affair, and he's not grieved, that would be abnormal. And this is how God means He is a jealous God (Exodus 20:5).

A normal, even godly, response is to be distressed by a wandering spouse. Now the defect of jealousy is when a person is being faithful, and their spouse is constantly mistrusting them. That's actually a kind of phobia that springs from insecurity.

People are often jealous and distrustful without cause. And I've seen this destroy marriages and otherwise positive relationships. That is a fault—a defect in human nature. So there are two sides of the jealousy coin. On one side there's an appropriate, normal jealousy from love and singleness of devotion. The other side is an abnormal jealousy from suspicion and fear.

In a sense, the Lord has married the church; we even take His name. And we take His name in vain when we call ourselves Christians and worship other gods. He has a right to be jealous if we decide to give our devotion to other gods after we have professed to accept Him as our husband. He wants our loyalty because we have promised it to Him through repentance and baptism.

But the other form of jealousy … where a man follows his wife around and secretly checks her mail … that's a sickness born of mistrust.

The Creation of Jesus?

 Based on Colossians 1:15, many say Christ was created or born. Does this mean He's not deity?

I believe Colossians 1:15, which reads, "[Jesus] is the image of the invisible God, the firstborn of every creature," is a very clear reference about the awesome nature of Christ, which is a belief under attack even in many Christian churches. The Messianic prophecy in Psalm 89:27 also reads, "I will make him my firstborn, higher than the kings of the earth," showing that Christ was not the firstborn prior to the creation narrative in Genesis, but rather He was to be made firstborn after the Psalmist penned his words. "The firstborn of every creature" is explained in Colossians 1:18 as "the firstborn from the dead."

We can also use a modern-day example. In America, we call the president's wife First Lady, but that doesn't mean she was the first lady born. It merely designates her role in America. Colossians should be read in the same way.

The word firstborn in Greek does not mean first one given birth to. Instead, it means the one who has priority—the one who has first position. A more accurate translation might say, "Who is the image of the invisible God, the first of every creature, or the highest of every creature."

Another thing we need to remember is all of the times Jesus called Himself infinite. You can't ignore those Scriptures when understanding His nature! For instance, Christ said, "Before Abraham was, I am" (John 8:58). He also calls Himself the Alpha and Omega (Revelation 1:8). Jesus is from everlasting to everlasting (Isaiah 63:16; Psalm 90:2). And one of the best Scriptures to explain that Christ is eternal is in the gospel of John: "All things were made by him; and without him was not anything made that was made" (1:3). If Christ made everything that's made, He couldn't have made Himself. He's always existed!

Let's look at another verse where we find a similar problem. Many take John 3:16, which says, "his only begotten son," and say that Jesus was begotten. Yet these people forget that when the Holy Spirit came upon Mary, it was the first time that God was born as a man. Christ is the only one of the Godhead who became a man, and so that's one way you can look at this.

Also, when we translate from Greek the phrase "the first begotten" or "the only begotten" or "the firstborn," that word can be translated as "the one who has preeminence of every creature." It doesn't necessarily mean He was born. Does it mean that the Father has a womb and gave birth to Jesus? Of course, this is an utterly ridiculous idea, but it helps illustrate the trouble in taking some passages of Scripture too literally.

Jesus has always been and will always be. He is divine and one with the Father and the Holy Spirit. "Jesus Christ the same yesterday, and to day, and for ever" (Hebrews 13:8).

The Divine Power of Jesus?

 Did Jesus use His divine power to do only good on earth?

 Absolutely. However, it is important to keep the following in mind. Whenever He did use His divine power to glorify the Father in heaven, He only used that power that is also available to you and me—His people. Jesus said, "The miracles I have done, greater things than this will you do because I will go on to the Father. As the Father sent me, so sent I you." Christ raised the dead, and His apostles raised the dead. He also healed and taught people, and He instructed His disciples to do that same.

Christ also never used His supernatural power for any selfish reasons. He could have used His power to save Himself. He could have refreshed Himself from sleepiness when He lay in the boat, but He chose to remain tired. He could have used His power while He was thirsting on the cross, but He had a greater mission than Himself.

Christ Tempted with Suicide?

 In Matthew 4:6, did Satan tempt Christ to commit suicide?

The verse reads, "And [the devil] saith unto him, If thou be the Son of God, cast thyself down: for it is written, He shall give his angels charge concerning thee: and in their hands they shall bear thee up, lest at any time thou dash thy foot against a stone" (Matthew 4:6).

The three temptations Jesus faced encompass every temptation that any of us face. We find in 1 John 2:16 that there are three basic temptations: lust of the flesh, lust of the eyes, and pride of life. Eve and Adam fell in those three areas; Christ overcame in those same three areas. We're all tempted by those three things.

The devil tempts each of us with self-destruction, which is the temptation described in Matthew 4:6. Before I was a Christian, I toyed with suicide quite a bit. Without God, life has no purpose. Suicide, for the non-Christian, is logical thinking.

If there's no God, no purpose, no eternity, and if people are unhappy most of the time, then what's the sense in living?

The Christian, on the other hand, realizes that suicide does not usher anyone into a better dimension, but instead permanently seals any bad circumstances. If you're struggling, suicide doesn't make it better. Suicide seals it forever. There's no reversing those bad circumstances.

Generally speaking, suicide is the last resort of a person who is in a faithless and hopeless condition. When such a person kills himself, all he has to look forward to is the resurrection of the damned. His next conscious thought is not a better one, but a worse one. The biggest lie of all is that suicide is going to be an escape. The Bible says sin is a transgression of God's law, and one of those commandments says, "Thou shalt not kill [murder]" (Exodus 20:13). That would include killing yourself.

Having said this, let me hasten to add that we must be careful not to automatically assume that all persons who have committed suicide will be lost. We may be surprised to find some in the kingdom who ended their own lives when they were not in their right minds due to unusual circumstances such as mental illness, chemical imbalance, or excruciating physical pain. We can trust God, who looks on the heart, to judge fairly in these cases.

Our lives are a sacred gift from God. The devil is using a lot of methods today to tempt people to self-destruction. Sometimes people commit suicide quickly; some do it by degrees through drugs, self-abuse, or cigarettes.

As long as you're a Christian, you've got hope—of new life, a new body, and eternal life. Just read your Bible and keep claiming God's promises. He'll get you through it.

The Two Natures of Man?

 How does one walk after the spirit and not the flesh according to Romans 8?

A. Christians have two natures that are at war within us—the spirit and the flesh. The selfish carnal, or physical, desires of the flesh want to be satisfied selfishly. However, the spirit strives to be pure, do God's will, and obey His commandments. The latter is the higher nature we should aim to please.

Peter and other New Testament writers speak about this war between the spirit and the flesh. And in Romans 8, Paul is encouraging Christians to walk after our spiritual natures and not our fleshly desires. You can read how Paul describes this often-difficult battle in Romans 7. I believe there is a simple, but not always easy, solution to this dilemma.

Here is a crude but effective illustration: Imagine you have two male dogs of the same breed. You feed one of your dogs the very best dog food, and you pet and groom him for attention, take him out for walks for exercise, and provide plenty of fresh water and rest. But the other dog you chain to a post, don't provide food, water, exercise, or attention at any time. Now imagine releasing the two dogs in the same area. Eventually, they'll do battle for the territory. Who will win? It's easy to guess that the dog that is well nourished and exercised will conquer the starved animal.

It's the same with the battle between our natures. The way you win the battle is decided in advance by which nature you choose to feed. If we feed the spirit by reading God's Word, spending time in prayer, fellowshiping with like-minded Christians, and sharing our faith, you will strengthen the spiritual aspect of your nature and make more room for the Holy Spirit. It's exactly like a muscle that gets bigger and stronger when you use it.

However, if you choose to feed your fleshly nature with worldly amusements and sensual gratification, your carnal nature will be on the throne and your spirit will lose the battle. There are so many distractions, shock television and other amoral entertainments, to compete. And Satan will do anything to make you fail. "But as then he that was born after the flesh persecuted him that was born after the spirit, *even so it is now*" (Galatians 4:29, emphasis added). The devil uses carnal reading materials, music, and television, often disguising it as "family entertainment," to tempt us and numb our spiritual walk. But these instant satisfactions have potentially terrible eternal consequences. They'll make your spiritual muscles limp and weak.

When temptation comes, whatever side we strengthen will win the battle. And every day, we're making a series of little decisions to walk after the flesh or the spirit. Pray daily, even hourly, for God's protection and always be mindful when investing time and resources into worldly amusements. Real satisfaction is found in the Prince of Peace, and not in the empty amusements of this world.

Men as Gods?

 John 10:34 is quite puzzling. It seems to say that men are gods.

Let's back up just one verse to John 10:33. Jesus is debating with some religious leaders about His deity. They're angry with Christ because He says to them, "I am the Son of God." They respond angrily in verse 33, saying, "For a good work we stone thee not; but for blasphemy; and because that thou, being a man, makest thyself God." Then Jesus answers, "Is it not written in your law, I said, Ye are gods?" I believe Jesus is referring to a quote from Psalm 82:6. Here the Lord is talking through King David, saying, "I have said, Ye are gods; and all of you are children of the most High."

Now you notice that in John 10 and in Psalm 82:6, the word gods begins with a lowercase "g." The writers of these books were not saying that men are divine. Though we were made in His image, we certainly do not possess the attributes of God. God is omnipotent (all-powerful), He's omnipresent (everywhere), and He's omniscient (knows all things). Humans are neither omniscient, omnipresent, or omnipotent—they aren't anything like the one true God. In addition, God is self-existent and eternal, whereas man is not.

When the Lord says, "You are gods," it means that God made man (Adam) in His own image. In the same way that God rules the universe, providing, leading, and governing, God originally made man to be the ruler of this planet. Man was to be the leader of this planet, having all the things of this world, like the fish and cattle, under his dominion. Man was made to rule this world, and God placed him here in His own image in the same way that the Father creates life. Man and woman were given the ability to procreate in their own image—out of an act of love, they can produce another human being in their likeness. In these ways, man is described as a lesser god of this world—but we certainly are not divine!

Living to See the Kingdom of God?

 Explain Matthew 16:28 about some not dying until they see the kingdom.

If you go to Mark 9, it's the same story. I like Mark's version a little better, because it gets right to the point. In Mark 9:1, Jesus said, "Verily I say unto you, That there be some of them that stand here, which shall not taste of death, till they have seen the kingdom of God come with power."

The way that verse is translated from the Greek means, "You are going to see a presentation of the kingdom coming." After that statement comes the fulfillment of what He's talking about.

"And after six days Jesus taketh with him Peter, and James, and John, and leadeth them up into an high mountain apart by themselves: and he was transfigured before them. And his raiment became shining, exceeding white as snow; so as no fuller on earth can white them" (Mark 9:2, 3).

Jesus was glorified. Moses, who represents those who died and are resurrected, was there. Elijah was there, representing those who are translated without seeing death. God the Father comes in a cloud and says, "This is my beloved Son" (verse 7).

What they saw was a miniature picture of the second coming. In Matthew 16:28 and Mark 9:1, Jesus was saying, "Before some of you die, you'll see what it will be like when I come to earth the second time."

The Woman's Seed Bruising the Serpent's Head?

 Explain the reference in Genesis 3:15 about the woman's seed bruising the serpent's head.

The Lord gives a prophecy to Eve, who is a symbol of the church; saying that "her seed," (her descendant, Jesus, and His followers), would bruise the head of the serpent, but the serpent would bruise His heel.

The only way to kill a serpent is to smash its head. And the word "bruise" there means to "smash" the head of the serpent. When a person is bruised on the heel, their progress is impeded. The devil has successfully hindered the progress of the Christian church, but it has not been a mortal wound. It has not stopped the church's motion.

I believe God was making a prophecy about a battle that would rage in our world between the serpent (the devil) and the woman (the church) from the day of mankind's fall in the Garden of Eden until Jesus returns.

In Revelation 12 you'll find a dragon (also called a serpent in verse 9) trying to devour a woman's baby as soon as the child is born (verse 4). This is the same serpent, Satan, who is called "the accuser of our brethren" (verse 10) and who persecutes "the woman who brought forth the man child" (verse 13).

Although Satan has been allowed to wound the heel of the woman, the prophecy in Genesis 3:15 adds that the woman and her seed, or offspring—which is Christ—would crush the serpent's head. At the cross, Jesus crushed the head of the serpent, the devil.

Have you ever noticed that when you kill a snake, it can still thrash around after its head has been crushed? It can still bite for a time also. The devil was crushed at the cross, but he's still thrashing around, snapping his jaws, and squirting venom. Not until our Lord returns will the church be fully freed from the torment of this defeated foe.

The Trinity?

 Would you explain the trinity?

This is a subject that has been debated by the greatest minds in Christendom for about 2,000 years. When mortal man tries to describe God, all he can do is make his best attempt. The Lord tells us, "For as the heavens are higher than the earth, so are my ways higher than your ways, and my thoughts than your thoughts" (Isaiah 55:9). If you and I could reach the stars, then maybe we could explain God. But we can't.

The Bible does, however, tell us enough so that we don't have to doubt. God is one unit of three persons. "God" is a family word; He consists of God the Father, God the Son, and God the Holy Spirit. In John 3:16 we see that God the Father sent God the Son in the form of a human that we might be forgiven.

At Jesus' baptism, you see these individuals again. The Father speaks from heaven saying, "This is my beloved son." The Spirit comes down in the form of a dove upon the Son. You've got the Father, the Son, and the Holy Spirit right there.

Some people are confused because Moses says, "Hear, O Israel: The LORD our God is one LORD" (Deuteronomy 6:4). The Bible also says that "God said, Let us make man in our image" (Genesis 2:26). We need to understand the Hebrew context of oneness. Moses wrote, "A man shall leave his father and mother and be joined to his wife, and they shall become one flesh" (Genesis 2:24 NKJV). Speaking of the apostles, Jesus prayed "that they all may be one; as thou, Father, art in me, and I in thee, that they also may be one in us" (John 17:21). The word "one" in the Bible doesn't just mean one person; it can also mean one in unity, or in purpose.

Galatians 4:4–6 states: "But when the fulness of the time was come, God sent forth his Son … To redeem them that were under the law, that we might receive the adoption of sons. And because ye are sons, God hath sent forth the Spirit of his Son into your hearts, crying, Abba, Father."

Here you have God the Father sending the Son and sending the Spirit that we might reflect God the Son. There are many different titles used in the Bible for God, but there is only one God who is united in His purpose of saving you and me. That's the trinity.

Bring Peace or a Sword?

Q. Explain how Jesus can leave us peace, but also say He came to bring not peace but a sword (Matthew 10:34)?

A. In Matthew 10:34, when Jesus says, "Think not that I come to send peace on earth," He means: "I did not come to bring political peace." The Word of God brings division. Hebrews 4:12 says, "For the word of God is quick, and powerful, and sharper than any twoedged sword." Christ is portrayed in Revelation as coming with a sword protruding from His mouth—a symbol of the Word of God. The Word of God can be divisive because people take different positions. But the salvation that Christ offers individually brings peace to those who receive His Word.

Genuine Christians—true Christians who lived godly lives through history—have been persecuted. Soft Christians, those who claim His name but don't live according to His Word, through history have been the persecutors. The Crusades that were fought, the Inquisition, and a lot of things that have happened through history—were started and carried out by "Christians" who were not really converted. They usually end up giving the genuine Christians a bad reputation. That, in turn, leads to further persecution of real Christians who have the teachings of Christ in their lives. And so in that sense, Christianity does not bring peace environmentally. It brings peace internally.

Section 2
The Nature of Sin and Salvation

The Pre-Commandment Moral Code?

Q. How did the Israelites have moral standards before the Ten Commandments? How did they know how to behave?

A. Before the Ten Commandments were written down in stone, the Bible tells us that the law was written in the hearts of the people. In addition, it was transmitted orally from father to son.

However, by the time of Moses, after the people had been in slavery under Egypt, and thereby under the influence of the Egyptian pagan religion, their memory had been somewhat corrupted and diluted.

That's why Moses wrote the first five books of the Bible, so his people would not be confused. Of course, God ultimately wrote the Ten Commandments so there would never have to be any guessing about what is right and wrong.

To prove this point: Long before Moses wrote the Ten Commandments onto scrolls, God said to Cain; "If you do well, will you not be accepted? And if you do not do well, sin lies at the door (Genesis 4:7 NKJV). The Bible also records, "Abraham obeyed my voice, and kept my charge, my commandments, my statutes, and my law" (Genesis 26:5). And not only did Abraham obey God's law, statutes, and commandments, Joseph knew it was a sin to commit adultery with Potiphar's wife. He said, "How then can I do this great wickedness, and sin against God" (Genesis 39:9). He evidently knew adultery was a sin long before the Ten Commandments were written. It had been passed on, so he knew what God's law was.

Originally, God's law went from Adam orally, straight out of the Garden of Eden, to become part of the oral tradition. In addition, Adam and Even were created in the image of God, so they knew their Father's character, which is revealed in the Ten Commandments. They passed this knowledge to their offspring, but because of man's failing memory, they eventually had to write it down.

Can You "Think" a Sin?

 Can a thought be a sin? Some say thoughts aren't sins unless you put them into action, but I'm not sure.

What I or someone else thinks about thoughts isn't worth much, but let's see what Jesus says about it. In Matthew 5:21, 22, our Lord says, "Ye have heard that it was said ... Thou shalt not kill; and whosoever shall kill shall be in danger of the judgment: But I say unto you, That whosoever is angry with his brother without a cause shall be in danger of the judgment." He's not actually calling someone like this a murderer, but He's discussing the importance about thinking angry thoughts.

Now jump down to verse 27. "Ye have heard that it was said ... Thou shalt not commit adultery: But I say unto you, That whosoever looketh on a woman to lust after her hath committed adultery with her already in his heart." Here the

Lord is telling us that sin is not always an action, it's an attitude. It's thoughts.

In the Sermon on the Mount, our Lord spent a lot more time talking about the attitude of pride and arrogance and sinful thoughts than the actual deeds, because every sinful deed originates with a thought in the mind. So if we're going to squelch sin, we need to begin by asking the Lord to get our minds and our thoughts captive to the Holy Spirit. That's where all sin originates.

Blaspheme the Holy Spirit?

Q. **What does it mean to blaspheme against the Holy Spirit? How do we know we haven't committed this "unpardonable sin"?**

A. Jesus speaks in Matthew 12:31, 32, about blasphemy against the Holy Spirit. He says, "All manner of sin and blasphemy will be forgiven man, except blasphemy against the Holy Spirit." Now this blasphemy against the Holy Spirit does not mean you lose your temper, shake your fist at God, and call Him names. That is certainly an outrageous sin, but that is not the "blasphemy against the Holy Spirit" of which Jesus is speaking.

The Jewish leaders accused Jesus of blasphemy when He claimed equality with God and the right to forgive sin. Of course, they would have been correct to do so if Jesus were not God.

However, blasphemy against the Holy Spirit is a perpetual, constant resisting of the drawing love of God's Spirit, so much so that you lose the capacity to hear the Holy Spirit's voice. The conscience becomes seared (1 Timothy 4:2). This deadly blasphemy is also called "grieving away" the Holy Spirit. Paul refers to "Grieve not the Holy Spirit, wherewith you are sealed," meaning we can permanently grieve away the Spirit.

Eventually, a person loses the capacity to repent, and therefore cannot be saved. It is for this sin that a person cannot be forgiven, because they have rejected the Spirit that convicts of sin (John 16:8). So if we still feel convicted of sin and have the desire to repent, then we have probably not committed the unpardonable sin.

Can Sins be Inherited?

 When a baby sins, is it because of his or her own sin or Adam's inherited sin?

A baby is not born with a sinful record, but every human is born with a sinful nature. We all have sinful tendencies. This question really might be addressing the concept of original sin.

This is kind of a loaded question, because a baby is obviously not born with a sinful record. If a baby in a Christian family should die, those parents will see that baby in the resurrection. But if the baby lives on, we know what happens. The Bible says, "All have sinned." Now this means committed sin. That baby, eventually, will understand the difference between right and wrong and will choose wrong at some point because that's what our sinful nature leads us to do.

Some have also wondered what the age of accountability is, and some churches have attempted to set an age. But the Bible is not specific on this subject. However, in the wilderness experience, those who did not believe perished in the wilderness—and this included anybody that was 20 years or older. I don't believe you could fight in the army until you were 20 years of age.

And in the Jewish culture, a boy is considered a man when he turns 12. He can go to the temple and participate in the services. So I would conclude that accountability is somewhere between 10 and 20, the age in which a young man or woman becomes accountable for sin. Incidentally, this would also be an appropriate age for baptism, because the Lord wants us to know what we're committing to. The Bible says that to be baptized, a person needs to repent, confess, accept, believe, be taught—and a baby can't do that. But a young child, somewhere between 10 and 15, begins to comprehend those things.

People often wonder about Jesus' state as a baby as well, so it's important that I address that too. He was born with a clean record—and every baby on entrance into this world is sparkling clean as far as the record of sin. However, we are born selfish creatures.

Jesus was born with the same potential to sin that you and I wrestle with. That's why the Bible says He was "tempted in all points, even as we are." The only difference is this: He didn't sin. That's why He can be our high priest and an advocate. He, through trusting the Father and by the grace of God, never did sin even though He was tempted just like we're tempted.

But He was not born as some kind of superman—immune to any kind of contamination. He knew what it was like to wrestle with temptation, but He never gave in, giving us an example that if He could overcome by trusting the Father, we can overcome by trusting Him. In essence, the Bible does not teach the concept of original sin. We are all responsible for our own actions.

A Gathering of Eagles?

What does Jesus mean in Matthew 24:28 and Luke 17:37 when He says, "For wherever the carcass is, there the eagles will be gathered together"?

First, the word "eagles" as used here is better translated as vultures or birds of carrion. In the last days, the Bible speaks about a feast of birds, which you can read about in Revelation 19:17, 18. It tells us that when the Lord comes, a time of great judgment for the wicked will occur. At one time, it was considered a curse of God for the deceased not to have their remains buried properly (1 Samuel 17:44, 46). It can be paralleled to the Flood recorded in Genesis, because it too was a judgment on the wicked. Remember Noah sent out a raven, and the raven did not come back because ravens are birds of carrion, but the dove he sent out later came back because it didn't have to anything to eat. It returned with an olive leaf in its mouth, which is now a symbol for peace.

But Jesus is referring to the next great and final judgment that is going to come on the wicked of the world. In Thessalonians 4, the saints are caught up to meet the Lord in the air and the dead in Christ rise. But we read that the wicked are destroyed by the brightness of His coming. Then Jeremiah 25:33 explains that after the return of the Lord, the carcasses of the wicked will be from one end of the earth to the other. They'll be no one to lament or to mourn them.

Must I Be Baptized to be Saved?

Q. Because of a certain medical condition, if I get water above my head, I'll die instantly. What happens if I hadn't been baptized yet?

A. The Bible says, "He that believeth and is baptized shall be saved; but he that believeth not shall be damned" (Mark 16:16). This is pretty powerful evidence that we all need to be baptized. But let me assure you that there are going to be a lot of people in heaven who couldn't be baptized.

I have visited a number of people on their deathbeds. I saw a gentleman dying from AIDS who gave his heart to the Lord; we prayed together. However, there was no way in the world he could go through a baptism. I've also visited people on death row. Some gave their lives to Jesus, but they couldn't get baptized because of the circumstances in prison. I believe that when Jesus was baptized, He was not baptized to wash away His own sins. I believe that we can claim for those individuals the credit of Christ's baptism. Think about the thief on the cross; he wasn't baptized, but Jesus guaranteed he would be in heaven after the resurrection.

If a person wants to be baptized but isn't able to, it isn't an obstacle to their salvation. The Lord is merciful. There are people out there who have physical challenges that make it very hard to be baptized. However, I've also baptized people in my church with a whole variety of challenges—we've had people we've actually carried into the baptistery because they wanted to be baptized so desperately. The Lord will find a way if we just have faith.

Are the 144,000 the Only Ones Saved?

 Who are the 144,000? Are they the only ones saved?

First, about 99 percent of all the information on the 144,000 is found primarily in Revelation 7 and 14. There are many strange ideas regarding this special group of people, so one must be careful when dealing with this subject matter. In that light, it's also important to note that I don't believe that this is an issue of salvation, but it is still a very important one.

Many people believe that because the Bible says the 144,000 are not defiled for they are virgins, it must mean that all 144,000 must be virgins. However, I believe the term "virgin" here is a symbol for the theologically pure. It means that they are not defiled with the false doctrines of the woman in Revelation 17.

The 144,000 are also not the only ones saved; they're not even the only ones saved in the last days. In chapter 7, there is a great multitude that no man can number. So the 144,000 represent a special group, the same way the 12 apostles were specially chosen by the Lord, filled with the Spirit, and commissioned to work for Him. In the last days, the Lord is going to have not 12 apostles—but 12 times 12,000! They will do a similar work of preaching the gospel around the world before the second coming. The Lord also said that there would be a special position for the 12 apostles, saying they would sit on 12 stones, reigning with Him (Luke 22:30). In the same way, Revelation 14 is saying there's a special position, a special relationship, for these 144,000 last-day people who are filled with the Spirit and working for the Lord.

The Sins of the Father?

 Are specific sins and their punishments passed down in families through the generations?

In the second commandment God says: "For I the LORD thy God am a jealous God, visiting the iniquity of the fathers upon the children unto the third and fourth generation of them that hate me; and shewing mercy unto thousands of them that love me, and keep my commandments" (Exodus 20:5, 6).

Is God is saying, "I'm going to place a curse on people and their children and great-grandchildren"? No. The Lord is explaining a life principal—parents reproduce their negative behaviors in their children. And you can usually trace it for three or four generations.

God does not arbitrarily impose your sin on your children. The Bible says very carefully, "The son is not accountable for the sins of the father, and the father is not accountable for the sins of the son. The righteousness of the righteous will be upon them. The wickedness of the wicked will be upon them." In another time, the Lord said, "Though Noah, Daniel, and Job were in the land, they will deliver neither son nor daughter by their righteousness. They will deliver their own souls."

God does not reward or punish offspring because of what the parents do. What He's saying in these passages is that, by the example of the parents, there's a strong probability that the children are going to follow that example. A good instance of this in the Bible is when the kingdom of Israel split. Jeroboam and the children of Israel in the north stopped worshiping at the temple of God. By his example, his children started to pray to idols, and then his grandchildren started to pray to idols, and so on—they lasted four generations and then they were destroyed. The same sort of thing happened again and again. Not because God cursed them, but because it's so important for us as parents to be good examples. That's what God is impressing.

Will the Babies be Saved?

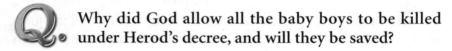

Why did God allow all the baby boys to be killed under Herod's decree, and will they be saved?

Jeremiah 31:15–17 indicates that the babies Herod murdered will be resurrected: "Rahel weeping for her children refused to be comforted for her children, because they were not. … saith the LORD; and they shall come again from the land of the enemy. … thy children shall come again to their own border." The Bible also seems to teach that children, before the age of accountability, are sanctified by believing parents (1 Corinthians 7:14). However, I don't know if God has a standard law that says that all babies who die before the age of accountability will be resurrected.

Many people wonder why God allows the innocent to suffer. A tyrant called the devil has kidnapped this world, and he does not play by the rules. The world rejected the leadership of God when Adam and Eve sinned. Now God intervenes only when we pray and ask Him to. Even Jesus referred to the devil as "the prince of this world" (John 14:30).

During the temptation in the wilderness in Matthew 4:9, the devil took Jesus up to a high mountain and showed Him all the kingdoms, "All these things will I give thee, if thou wilt fall down and worship me."

Satan claims this world as his own. So it should not surprise us when we see the innocent suffering at the hands of the wicked here in this world. Remember that the penalty of sin is death, but God, in His mercy, has not executed the planet because He's seeking to save as many as He can. So instead of asking the question, "Why do innocent people like the babies in Bethlehem suffer?" we ought to be asking, "Why is God so merciful that He sought to preserve and save so many?"

Should We Judge Other Christians?

Does the Bible say we should judge sin in other Christians?

 Jesus said, "Judge not according to the appearance, but judge righteous judgment" (John 7:24). He also tells us that we can know if a person is genuine or not by their fruit. "Ye shall know them by their fruits ... Wherefore by their fruits ye shall know them" (Matthew 7:16, 20). The text that people often quote to hide from the evaluations of others is, "Judge not, that ye be not judged" (Matthew 7:1). That's not how Jesus meant that text to be used. A parallel verse in Luke provides more details. "Judge not, and ye shall not be judged: condemn not, and ye shall not be condemned: forgive, and ye shall be forgiven" (6:37). Jesus meant that we should not condemn and pass judgment on people.

The Bible tells us that we are our brother's keeper. We are to care about one another. James tells us that if we see a brother who is going astray, those who are spiritual should try to bring him back again. "If any of you do err from the truth, and one convert him; Let him know, that he which converteth the sinner from the error of his way shall save a soul from death, and shall hide a multitude of sins" (James 5:19, 20). It's understood from that passage that we are to intervene if we know a person is erring in their ways. Matthew shows the proper method for approaching someone who is in error. "Moreover if thy brother shall trespass against thee, go and tell him his fault between thee and him alone: if he shall hear thee, thou hast gained thy brother. But if he will not hear thee, then take with thee one or two more, that in the mouth of two or three witnesses every word may be established" (18:15, 16). The Bible says some very strong things about Christians using good judgment and patient love in dealing with each other.

Once Saved, Always Saved?

I hear a lot of people preaching "once saved, always saved," but I'm pretty sure this isn't biblical. I was wondering if there are Bible verses that talk about losing salvation.

Many Bible verses explain that people are saved based upon a choice they make and sustain. One of the most powerful texts is found in Ezekiel 18:24, which says, "When the righteous turneth away from his righteousness, and committeth iniquity, and doeth according to all the abominations that the wicked man doeth, shall he live? All his righteousness that he hath done shall not be mentioned: in his trespass that he hath trespassed, and in his sin that he hath sinned, in them shall he die."

The Scriptures make it clear that salvation isn't a choice we simply make one day and then go our own way. When we accept salvation, we are making a free choice, and if we later choose to reject God, we are given that freedom as well. Just as the devil cannot force anybody to be lost, so Jesus does not force anybody to be saved. We must choose to serve Him.

Many people get confused because the Lord says that He will not lose or let go of anyone that comes to Him (John 6:37). What this means is that He will never turn His back on us. It does not mean that He will save individuals who stop coming to Him! Knowing that it is possible for us to lose our salvation, Paul counsels in Hebrews 10:23, "Let us hold fast the profession of our faith without wavering."

The idea of "once saved, always saved" can be traced to John Calvin. While he was a great theologian, this particular doctrine is not biblical. For example, the New Testament tells of Demus, Paul's friend who traveled with him but later threw off his salvation to go back into the world (2 Timothy 4:10). In the Old Testament, we have the example of King Saul, who was chosen by God and anointed and filled with the Holy Spirit but later turned his back on God and committed suicide (1 Samuel 10; 1 Chronicles 10:13).

Many Christians believe that if an individual falls back into sin, it is because that person was never truly saved. However, accepting Christ as our Savior never guarantees that we will be free from temptations to turn away from Him or that we will no longer have the freedom to decide our eternal destinies. To suggest that once we're saved we can't be lost is like saying that the Lord holds us as hostages against our will, and He would never do that! It is true that once we're in heaven we will never be lost, but in this world we are still in a land of war, and we can defect to the enemy any time we want.

Of course, choosing sin after knowing salvation can bring only great pain. Peter warns: "If after they have escaped the pollutions of the world through the knowledge of the Lord and Saviour Jesus Christ, they are again entangled therein, and overcome, the latter end is worse with them than the beginning. For it had been better for them not to have known the way of righteousness, then, after they have know it, to turn from the holy commandment delivered unto them" (2 Peter 2:20–22).

As you can see, countless Scriptures explain that salvation is based on a daily commitment. That's why Paul said, "I die daily" (1 Corinthians 15:31), meaning that He put his human nature to death each day so that he could live for the Lord.

Instead of taking our salvation for granted, we must heed Matthew 24:13, which says, "But he that shall endure unto the end, the same shall be saved." Furthermore, as 1 Corinthians 10:12 warns, "Let him that thinketh he standeth take heed lest he fall."

Of course, we must not make the opposite mistake of being so constantly fearful that we fall into a yo-yo, saved-lost-saved-lost relationship with God! The Bible doesn't condone that either.

While it is true that people who are saved may sin, they are instantly grieved and led to repentance by the Holy Spirit. As Romans 8:14, 15, promises: "For as many as are led by the Spirit of God, they are the sons of God. For ye have not received the spirit of bondage again to fear; but ye have received the Spirit of adoption, whereby we cry, Abba, Father." By daily continuing our walk with Christ, we can have assurance and confidence of our salvation.

In God We Trust?

 Is it wrong to expect God's protection when facing calamity?

A. Don't go out and chase a tornado and assume that God will protect you. We ought to do what we can to avoid calamity, and then ask God to protect us and expect that we can have peace. Christians are not immune to calamity—look at Job, for instance—but God does protect those who trust in Him. There are a number of promises in the Bible, Psalm 91 for instance, that offer a lot of comfort and encouragement regarding calamity and God's protection in those environments. Look at the story of Shadrach, Meshach, and Abednego who went into the fiery furnace. They said, "Our God whom we serve is able to deliver us from the burning fiery furnace, and he will deliver us out of thine hand, O king. But if not, be it known unto thee, O king, that we will not serve thy gods" (Daniel 3:17, 18). God did deliver them. And more times that not, God does protect His own from harm.

Where Does the Spirit Go When We Die?

Q. Does the spirit go straight to God or does it stay with our bodies after we have died?

A. First of all, keep in mind what the Bible means by the world "spirit." In Hebrew and Greek, this word means "the breath of life." For instance, Ecclesiastes 12:7 says, "Then shall the dust return to the earth as it was: and the spirit shall return unto God who gave it." The "spirit" is not referring to the consciousness or living soul, but to the actual breath. The next thought that a saved person has after he or she dies is the resurrection.

The Bible says that, "In a moment, in the twinkling of an eye, at the last trump: for the trumpet shall sound, and the dead shall be raised incorruptible, and we shall be changed" (1 Corinthians 15:52).

Everyone knows the resurrection takes place when Jesus returns, but this is where confusion often arises. Some people believe that 2 Corinthians 5:8, "We are confident, I say, and willing rather to be absent from the body, and to be present with the Lord," and 1 Thessalonians 4:16, "For the Lord himself shall descend from heaven with a shout … and the dead in Christ shall rise first" cannot both be correct.

However, the first passage is often misinterpreted. It is simply saying that faith (see verses 6, 7) leads us to long for the day when the work of spreading the gospel on earth is finished so that He can come again and take us home to heaven. So which verse is true? They both are!

Jesus tells us that death is a sleep. For example, in John 11:11, Jesus told his followers and disciples, "Our friend Lazarus sleepeth; but I go, that I may awake him out of sleep." Look down a bit further in the passage. Notice that Martha is skeptical, and she answers, "I know that he shall rise again at the resurrection at the last day" (verse 24).

Perhaps the most clear verses on the condition of the dead are Ecclesiastes 9:5, 6: "For the living know that they shall die: but the dead know not any thing, neither have they any more a reward; for the memory of them is forgotten. Also their love, and their hatred, and their envy, is now perished; neither have they any more a portion for ever in any thing that is done under the sun."

John 5:28, 29, provides an excellent summary of earth's last day. "Marvel not at this: for the hour is coming, in the which all that are in the graves shall hear his voice, And shall come forth; they that have done good, unto the resurrection of life; and they that have done evil, unto the resurrection of damnation."

Keeping the Law for Love or Salvation?

Could you explain keeping the law out of love, rather than keeping it to be saved?

A. Probably the best illustration for this concept is the Exodus experience. When Moses went to Egypt to lead the children of Israel out of slavery, God tested their faith by requiring them to offer the Passover lamb. This signified that they were saved from slavery based upon their faith in the blood of the lamb. They needed to be both filled with the lamb and covered by its blood before they began their journey.

Next God brought the Israelites to Mount Sinai. A lot of people start the first commandment with "Thou shalt have no other gods before me" (Exodus 20:3), but this skips something important. The first words written on the tables of stone were: "I am the LORD thy God, which have brought thee out of the land of Egypt, out of the house of bondage" (verse 2). God was saying: "I saved you. Here's My law."

When Jesus said, "If ye love me, keep my commandments" (John 14:15), He was quoting from the third commandment, which says, "Shewing mercy unto thousands of them that love me, and keep my commandments" (verse 6). You cannot obey God's law unless you love Him first.

Would My Clone Go to Heaven?

Q. If I could be cloned, would both of me go to heaven?

A. Despite what you might have heard, it is impossible to stamp people out with a cookie-cutter mold. Cloning simply means taking the DNA from one living person and using it to make a second human being. The second person would always be younger than the first and would have his or her own unique identity. The cloned person would have completely different experiences and make different choices than the "original," because he would be a different person altogether. A clone would merely be someone who had the same genetic makeup as another person. As a matter of fact, twins share a similar situation.

Since the clone would be a different soul, he would need to make his own decision to accept God's gift of salvation. He would not automatically go to heaven.

An End to Evil?

 Why doesn't God stop evil?

I'm a parent. I'm bigger than my children, but I don't want them to listen to me simply because I overpower them with brute force. I want them to listen to me because they love me.

God is love (1 John 4:8). He does have the divine power to obliterate the devil and kill everyone who is evil, but if He had done that as soon as Lucifer sinned, His creatures would have been motivated by fear rather than by love. When Lucifer began to insinuate that God's government wasn't quite fair, the Lord had to stand back in order to let both angels and mortals witness this spectacle (1 Corinthians 4:9). He needed to demonstrate the result of Satan's government to the universe. The Lord grieves more than anyone about the sin and suffering in this world.

Jesus does not force us to love Him; He does not work that way. Love, real love, requires the freedom to choose.

Born Again by Water and the Spirit?

What does the Bible mean in John 3 about being born again by water and the Spirit? Is it essential to be baptized to be saved?

A. There will be many, many people in heaven who were never baptized. For example, almost all of the Old Testament characters would be in that category.

Notice what Mark 16:16 says: "He that believeth and is baptized shall be saved; but he that believeth not shall be damned." This verse does not say, "He that believes and is not baptized shall be damned." We have no record that the thief on the cross was baptized. He was saved by grace, through faith.

I've been to hospitals where people gave their heart to the Lord on their deathbed. They could not be baptized because they were attached to various apparatus. I believe Jesus gives people like the thief on the cross, folks dying in hospitals, and prisoners on death row credit for His baptism. Obviously, Christ was not baptized to wash away His sins. John the Baptist told Jesus, "You need to baptize me because You're sinless. Why am I baptizing You?" (Matthew 3:14, paraphrased). Christ was baptized as an example for us and on behalf of those who could not be. They receive credit for Christ's sinless life by virtue of faith.

My question is this: If a person believes in the Word of the Lord and knows that the Bible commands baptism, why wouldn't he want to be baptized? A person who knows God's will and refuses to do it is in a dangerous situation.

A Baptized Sinner or a Wet Devil?

Q. If a person wants to be baptized, must he first overcome his bad habits, or will the Holy Spirit help him with these problems after baptism? We repent of sin on a daily basis, don't we?

A. I believe that certain tangible life changes should be evident before baptism. This is why John the Baptist stated, "Bring forth therefore fruits meet for repentance"

(Matthew 3:8). Since baptism reflects new birth, new life, and liberation from a life of sin, being baptized while still enslaved to sinful habits such as drinking or smoking would be a paradox. Baptism is similar to marriage. For a man to marry a woman while still dating another would be hypocrisy. Similarly, a person shouldn't enter into a union with Christ through baptism while willingly still "dating the devil" in certain areas of life. I am not suggesting that an individual needs to know everything or to be perfect before baptism. However, no one should enter into this special relationship unrepentant. Evidence of Christ's victory will be apparent in a life that is consecrated to the Lord. Of course, baptism does not bring perfection, and new believers will certainly feel a need for repentance after baptism. Thankfully, we have the promise that "if any man sin, we have an advocate with the Father, Jesus Christ the righteous" (1 John 2:1). As we go to Him daily, asking for forgiveness and the power to do His will, we will grow to be more and more like our Savior.

... But Few Are Chosen

Q. My question is concerning Calvinism. Do you think that God has predestined from birth certain individuals to be saved and others not to be?

A. I think John Calvin was a tremendous Christian, and I expect to see him in the kingdom of heaven. As a theologian, he's often remembered for his writings on the topic of predestination.

Back in the 1700s, George Whitfield, a mighty preacher from England, had a very heated debate with Methodist ministers Charles and John Wesley over this subject. John and Charles Wesley did not believe in Calvin's view of predestination, but George Whitfield did. Finally the three

THE NATURE OF SIN AND SALVATION

men said: "We need to agree to disagree. Let's lay aside our differences on this issue and work for the salvation of others."

If the debate were taking place today, I would side with the Wesleys. The Bible tells us that God is "not willing that any should perish, but that all should come to repentance" (2 Peter 3:9). Predestination advocates interpret Matthew 22:14, which says that "many are called, but few are chosen," to mean that God has chosen some individuals to be saved and some not to be saved. It asserts that since the Bible says in Romans 9:13 that God loved Jacob and hated Esau, this means that He didn't want Esau to be saved. Therefore Esau was predestined to be lost.

I don't believe the Bible means that at all. I think that when the Lord says, "Many are called, but few are chosen," that could be translated as "many are called, but few respond." The many who are called are identified in John 3:16: "For God so loved the world, that he gave his only begotten Son, that whosoever believeth in him should not perish, but have everlasting life." In other words, you and I have been given a will, and we choose with our will whether or not to be saved.

In Revelation 22:17, Jesus said, "Whosoever will, let him come and take the water of life freely." As people line up for that water, Jesus doesn't say: "I'm sorry. I don't want you to drink from My fountain." The Lord wants everyone to be saved. He even wanted Judas to be saved.

John Calvin would have said that God decided Judas would be lost because He needed him to fit into the prophetic scheme. I disagree. God wanted Judas to be saved. In His omnipotent wisdom He could look ahead and see what Judas was going to do, but that does not mean that He made him betray Jesus. That's where the confusion comes in.

Try to picture a traffic helicopter hovering over a section of highway in which there are two lanes going opposite directions through a tunnel on top of a mountain. The person in the helicopter is looking down and sees that a little red Volkswagen is getting ready to pass an 18-wheeler inside the tunnel.

Coming up the other side of the mountain is another 18-wheeler in the oncoming lane. It hasn't happened yet, but that pilot can safely report that there's going to be an accident in the tunnel. The helicopter pilot is not making it happen, but he sees that it's going to happen. For someone to say that the pilot predestined the crash is ridiculous.

God knows all things. He does not want there to be a crash in the tunnel, but He sees it coming. A person needs to understand that God longs for everyone to be saved and wants all people to come to repentance. 1 Timothy 2:3, 4 declares, "For this is good and acceptable in the sight of God our Saviour; Who will have all men to be saved, and to come unto the knowledge of the truth." God is love (1 John 4:8), and He doesn't want any person to perish.

A New Planet Earth?

 Will this planet be the new earth after Jesus' second coming?

God had an original plan for this earth before He ever created it. His plan has been corrupted, perverted, and polluted by the devil. However, the devil is not going to able to ultimately confound God's plan. The Lord is going to create a new heaven (a new atmosphere!) and a new earth (Revelation 21:1).

He's going to take this same earth and recreate it, because the Bible says that "the meek ... shall inherit the earth" (Matthew 5:5). And furthermore, Christ says, "In my Father's house are many mansions: if it were not so, I would have told you. I go to prepare a place for you. And if I go and prepare a place for you, I will come again, and receive you unto myself; that where I am, there ye may be also" (John 14:2, 3). The righteous will be caught up to meet the Lord in the air (1 Thessalonians 4:17). Then they will spend a millennium in heaven, living and reigning with Christ (Revelation 20:4). Finally, the apostle John says, "I saw the holy city, new Jerusalem, coming down from God out of heaven" (Revelation 21:2). The New Jerusalem is the city of God, and its new home will be this planet. There will be no ozone depletion or greenhouse effect though. It will be this earth, made new.

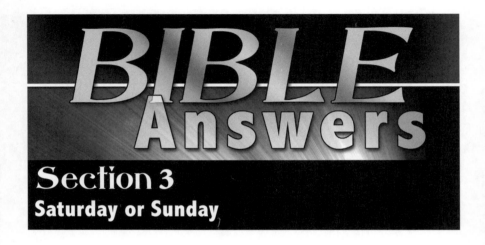

Section 3
Saturday or Sunday

Do I Have to Keep the Sabbath?

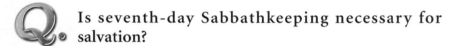

Q. Is seventh-day Sabbathkeeping necessary for salvation?

A. The Sabbath is one of the Ten Commandments. My approach toward the Sabbath commandment would be the same as my approach to the other nine. The question is whether or not we keep the commandments to be saved, or if we are keeping the commandments because we are saved. If I say that I am saved, but I'm stealing and I have a wife on each coast, then my relationship with the Lord is questionable, isn't it? There will be people in heaven who had several wives because they did not know the truth regarding this—consider King David, Solomon, and Abraham. That doesn't mean that God condones polygamy. In the same way, there will be people in heaven who went to church on Sunday, and maybe those who didn't go to church at all, because they didn't know the truth about God's holy day. But when a person knows God's will in any of these areas and says, "I'm not going to obey this or that commandment for my own reasons," then the Bible's message is clear—if we sin willfully after we receive a knowledge of the

44

truth, then Jesus' blood doesn't cover us. "For if we sin wilfully after that we have received the knowledge of the truth, there remaineth no more sacrifice for sins" (Hebrews 10:26). The idea that you can willfully break God's commandments and still be saved is not biblical.

Rest or Church on Sabbath?

Q. Exodus 16:29 seems to suggest that God wants us to stay home and rest on the Sabbath. If so, is it even necessary to go to church?

A. Let's first start by taking a look at Exodus 16:29: "Let every man remain in his place; let no man go out of his place on the seventh day."

The reason God told the Israelites to remain in their places was because they were out looking for bread on a day when God said there would be none. Exodus 16:27–29 says, "See! For the LORD has given you the Sabbath; therefore He gives you on the sixth day bread for two days." God was not suggesting that they sit in their tents for 24 hours. Furthermore, "in his place" really means in the camp. God did not want them out gathering sticks or bread, as that was work (Numbers 15:32). Of course, they did water, feed, and milk their flocks (Luke 13:15).

So yes, God very much wants us to gather for worship on the Sabbath, which is why the Sabbath is called a "Holy Convocation" in Leviticus 23:3—"Six days shall work be done, but the seventh day is a Sabbath of solemn rest, a holy convocation." Convocation means: "To convene, come together usually for an official or public purpose; assemble formally. A community who are assembled for a ceremony."

This was the example of Jesus, as we see in Luke 4:16. "So He came to Nazareth, where He had been brought up. And as His custom was, He went into the synagogue on the Sabbath day, and stood up to read. Even the word synagogue means to come together—Latin *synag ga,* from Greek *sunag g,* assembly, synagogue, from *sunagein,* to bring together.

Acts 13:44 shows that the disciples gathered in the synagogue for study on the Sabbath, and they also came together for prayer by the river. And on the next Sabbath, almost the entire city came together to hear the Word of God. "And on the Sabbath day we went out of the city to the riverside, where prayer was customarily made; and we sat down and spoke to the women who met there" (Acts 16:13).

One of the most important features of the Sabbath is when God's people come together for corporate worship. When we neglect to do this, we rob God of the collective worship He deserves and ourselves of the fellowship blessings we need. "Seven days without church makes one weak."

Pentecost—Which Day?

 What day was the Pentecost? Was it on Saturday or on Sunday?

I believe Pentecost occurred on what we would call Sunday. The root word "penta" means five or fifty; for example, the pentagon has five sides. Now after Passover, there are seven weeks, and after the last Passover Sabbath, which is the 49th day, comes the day Pentecost, or 50th day (Deuteronomy 16:9).

So Sunday must have been when the Pentecost took place. In fact, the disciples were beginning the work, as it was a customary workday then. They were beginning the work of spreading the gospel, just like Jesus rose on Sunday to continue His work as a High Priest. Christ rested in the tomb on the Sabbath and then commenced His work on our behalf when He rose Sunday morning.

Unfortunately, some people use the Pentecost as a justification for going to church on Sunday and ignore the Sabbath as a holy day. But that is quite a stretch. There is nothing in the Bible that says to keep Pentecost, Sunday, or even the day of Jesus' resurrection holy.

By that logic, we could keep Thursday as the Sabbath because that's when the Lord instituted the New Covenant at the Lord's Supper. You could even argue that it should be Friday, because that's when Jesus was crucified.

But nowhere in the Bible does God pick any other day to replace the seventh day of the week. So I think it's pretty reckless for Christians to start altering the law of God, the one He spoke with His voice and wrote with His finger. Jesus said, "Why do ye also transgress the commandment of God by your tradition?" (Matthew 15:3).

Show me a Scripture that says, "Keep the first day as the Sabbath," and I'll do just that. But until I find that, are we going to take men's traditions over the very clear Word of God?

The Bible says that the Lord blessed and sanctified the seventh day. He wrote it in stone with His finger; He spoke it with His voice, saying, "Remember," meaning that we're not to forget it. We can't get away from the Word of God. "But in vain they do worship me, teaching for doctrines the commandments of men" (Matthew 15:9).

Which Day is the Sabbath?

Which day is the Sabbath? Has it been changed, and does it still matter today?

The Bible is very clear that the Sabbath is the seventh day of the week. "Remember the sabbath day, to keep it holy," God wrote in the Ten Commandments. "Six days shalt thou labour, and do all thy work: But the seventh day is the sabbath of the LORD thy God. … For in six days the LORD made heaven and earth, the sea, and all that in them is, and rested the seventh day: wherefore the LORD blessed the sabbath day, and hallowed it" (Exodus 20:8–11).

Many spiritual people worship Jesus on the first day of the week, believing that the Sabbath was meant for the Jews only. But is this true? In Genesis 2:1, 2, the Bible says that after the Lord created the world, "Thus the heavens and the earth were finished, and all the host of them. And on the seventh day God ended his work which he had made; and he rested on the seventh day from all his work which he had made. And God blessed the seventh day, and sanctified it: because that in it he had rested from all his work which God created and made." The Sabbath is a memorial of Creation, and Christ sanctified it in the very beginning. No Jews existed at the beginning of the world! God chose a day to remind not only the Jews, but all of humanity that He is both our sustainer and our Creator. God desires for all His children to rest and worship on the seventh day.

How do we know that the seventh day is what we call "Saturday"? First of all, Jews today still worship on Saturday. For a whole nation to forget which day is the Sabbath would be hard to believe! Second, astronomers who have studied changes in the calendar affirm that while many changes to the calendar have been made, they in no way affected the weekly cycle. Third, the Bible tells us that even in His death, Jesus rested on the Sabbath. He was crucified on what was called "Good Friday," the preparation day, and He rested in the tomb on the Sabbath and rose the first day of the week (Luke 23:50–56, 24:1–3). Fourth, dictionaries define "Sunday" as the first day of the week and "Saturday" as the seventh day. Indeed, if one looks at a calendar, the weeks begin with Sunday and end with Saturday. Fifth, in 145 languages of the world, the word for the seventh day of the week means "Sabbath day"!

The importance of the Sabbath has nothing to do with legalism; it has to do with love. All love relationships require time, and God knew we needed a special day on which to nurture our relationship with Him. The devil wants us to forget about that time of rest so that our relationship with God will be destroyed. However, God still calls us to "Remember the Sabbath day" (Exodus 20:8) and honor Him as Creator by setting it apart for Him each week.

The Sabbath vs. the Sabbaths?

 How does Galatians 4:9–11 relate to Sabbath observance?

The text reads: "But now, after that ye have known God, or rather are known of God, how turn ye again to the weak and beggarly elements whereunto ye desire again to be in bondage? Ye observe days, and months, and times, and years. I am afraid of you, lest I have bestowed upon you labour in vain" (Galatians 4:9–11). Paul also refers to this subject in Romans 14.

The Jewish people celebrated two very distinct kinds of holy days: the Sabbath of the Ten Commandments, which existed before sin took hold on this planet (see Genesis 2), and the sabbath days, which were ceremonial holy days established after sin.

The Sabbath of the Ten Commandments was spoken by God's voice; the other ceremonial sabbaths were spoken by Moses. The Fourth-Commandment Sabbath was written by God's finger in stone; the other holy days were written on parchment by Moses. When Jesus came, He fulfilled and nailed to the cross the ceremonial laws. He did not, however, wipe away the Ten Commandments. When we accept Jesus Christ, it doesn't mean that we have a license to lie, kill, and commit adultery. The Sabbath commandment is part of that same package.

When the apostle Paul wrote this passage, the Jewish converts to Christianity were telling the Galatians and the Romans to start observing the Passover, all of the Jewish holy days, the Day of Atonement, the Feast of Trumpets, and so forth. Paul was simply saying, "You are telling these people to observe the ceremonial shadows that pointed to Jesus. It doesn't make sense to worship a shadow when the real thing has already come." He wasn't referring to the Sabbath of the Ten Commandments.

Some have tried to convince people that God was abolishing the one commandment that begins with the word "Remember." It's a weak argument. I've never heard a Sunday-keeping pastor stand up and say, "Don't come to church on Sundays, or you'll be observing days!"

Sabbath Healing?

 Is it okay to work as a nurse on the Sabbath?

The Bible records that Jesus, by His example, shows that it is right to relieve suffering on the Sabbath, and that by relieving the afflicted we bring honor to His day.

However, that means that we are not to do unnecessary work, or anything that can be done another day. Because of the nature of nursing duties, some are tempted to feel justified in doing things on the Sabbath that aren't necessary. This can become habitual, until the sense of Sabbath sacredness is lost, and God's commandments are broken.

Some medical people perform services on the Sabbath so they will be free other days of the week to do their own thing. That, I believe, is consciously breaking God's commandment. There are times when we must take our turn, and emergencies can arise where we must do duty on the Sabbath, but the money we make on that day should be put in God's treasury. Many conscientious

Christians do this, and these God honors and blesses. God will guide you if you put your trust in Him (Proverbs 3:5, 6).

Sabbath Work?

What type of work is allowed on Sabbath?

Let's use Jesus as an example. The Bible says that Christ healed people on the Sabbath. "And it was the sabbath day when Jesus made the clay, and opened his eyes" (John 9:14). Jesus, by trade, was a carpenter. Do we ever see Him driving nails and building chairs and houses on the Sabbath? No. Do we see Him doing ministry of healing, feeding, and teaching on the Sabbath? Yes. "It is lawful to do well on the sabbath days" (Matthew 12:12). It's our regular work that we're to lay aside. The idea of the Sabbath is quality time with God to develop that love relationship.

BIBLE Answers

Satan Cast Away?

Q. Satan was cast away from heaven, so why do Job 1:6 and Revelation 12:7 seem to say he's got fairly easy access there?

A. Well, first of all, Satan was cast out of heaven after Adam and Eve chose to listen to the devil instead of God. The devil basically set up the earth as his staging grounds to fight God. Paul says earth is now a theater to the universe; we're a spectacle (1 Corinthians 4:9). The universe is watching what's happening here on this planet.

But when you get to Revelation 12, where it mentions the war between Michael and the dragon and how the dragon is cast out, it's not all regarding future prophecy. Some prophecy looks back, and this is an example of that. Satan did not just come to earth when Revelation was written. He started working and fighting man on earth with his fallen angels way back after man fell, so Revelation 12 is a prophetic picture looking backward.

I also believe Satan could have been cast out of heaven in degrees. When Christ completed His ministry and said, "It is finished," (John 19:30), Satan's access to heaven was even more limited. Yet Satan still works as an accuser of the faithful and in someway he can discourse with God. God is everywhere, so Satan here on earth can shake his fists at God in heaven and say, "You know the only reason Job serves you is because you protect him." Satan also accuses Joshua the high priest in Zechariah, so he still accuses God. But he can't go to the gates of heaven and tempt the angels of heaven anymore.

King David, a Man after God's Own Heart?

 Why did God allow David to keep Bathsheba as his wife?

David did suffer terribly because of his sin with Bathsheba. He lost four children, the first baby between him and Bathsheba, the fruit of their sinful and forbidden romance.

Absalom killed Amnon, and then was killed. And he lost yet another son. He also lost the respect of his people, and his reputation was besmirched.

But then David thoroughly repented. Keep in mind; he stayed on his face for seven days in repentance and grief for his sins—begging God for mercy. And God not only forgave him, He even blessed their relationship, as husband and wife, to show they had been truly forgiven. Furthermore, David's next child was also blessed to be the ancestor of the Messiah.

It would have been a cruel act for David to put away Bathsheba after the death of her husband and baby through his influence. And God not only forgave them, He even blessed their marriage. He gave them Solomon, which means "Peace." He not only became the next king, but he was also blessed as the ancestor of the Messiah.

It's much like the story of the Samaritan woman at the well. She'd been married five times and was living with another man.

Jesus forgave and accepted her even in the midst of her sin. He comes to us just as we are. Isn't that great news?

This is great evidence of God's grace and forgiveness. Suppose you make some terrible decision in your life that is irreversible. Does it mean you cannot be saved? Absolutely not! This story shows that God can redeem us even after we have wandered far off the path. Though He will not always reverse the consequences of our poor decisions, we may always return to Him.

Jacob's Wrestling Match

 With whom did Jacob wrestle? Was it an angel or was it God?

The word "angel" is used several different ways in the Bible. The name simply means messenger. In this story, it first appears that Jacob wrestles with an angel. But later, he says, "I have seen God," because of what the angel says to him. For instance, this messenger gives Jacob a new name. You read in Revelation that Jesus is the one who gives us new names, so I believe that Jacob wrestled with the pre-incarnate Son of God.

The story is that the Lord comes to visit Jacob, who is fearful that Esau and his commandoes are coming after him. More than a little tense, he prays in the darkness, but someone touches him. He spins around to overpower the stranger, but the inhuman strength of the visitor reveals that this is not a mere earthling—it isn't Esau, or even a human at all, but God. In the end, God says, "You have to let go because the day is breaking." Jacob answers, "I won't let you go unless you bless me." Of course, Jacob isn't presuming that he can out wrestle God; instead, he's pleading for mercy. He says to God, "I want to know my sins are forgiven before I let you go." In other words: "I'm not going to let go of my faith."

It's also important to clarify that Scriptures say, "No man has seen God" at any time. But you also see several places in the Old Testament where people talked to God—like Abraham and Moses. And now you have Jacob actually wrestling with the Almighty. Take Manoah and his wife when they see a messenger from heaven. They say, "We have seen God. We're going to die." Who is this messenger?

You know, Christ existed before His Bethlehem incarnation, which is why He says, "Before Abraham was, I Am." And I believe it was Christ who appeared many times to these patriarchs. In John's gospel, He says, "No man has seen God the Father." The member of the Godhead not seen by mortals is the Father, because many people have seen the Son.

The story also seems implicit in saying the two wrestled physically, and not just spiritually. Jacob didn't have Jesus in a "head lock", but he might have just latched on to the Lord's feet, trying to free himself until realizing He couldn't overcome the supernatural visitor. We also know that when the angel touched Jacob's thigh, it shrank and he hobbled the rest of his life. It was a divine touch, and he wrestled with God till sunrise.

Who is the Woman of Genesis 3:15?

 Who is the woman in Genesis 3:15? Is she Mary?

That Scripture is symbolically talking about the church—Eve is a symbol for the church. I believe God is making a prophecy about a battle that would rage in our world between the serpent, the devil, and the woman—the church from the Garden of Eden—until Jesus comes back. Go to Revelation 12, and you'll find the serpent trying to devour the baby of a woman. The serpent bruising the woman's heal in Genesis means the devil will impede the progress of the church by biting its heel. But it says that the woman—and later it says the seed of the woman and then later her baby, who is a symbol of Christ—would crush the serpent's head.

At the cross, Jesus crushed the head of the serpent—the devil. Snakes will thrash around awhile after you crush their heads, and they can still bite even after that point. The devil was crushed at the cross, but he's still thrashing around and snapping his jaws and squirting venom. His head was mortally crushed, but he has wounded the heel of the woman, the church in Jesus.

But don't take it from me alone! In the New Testament, Paul alludes to that passage indicating that the woman there in Genesis is speaking of the church.

What About the Brothers and Sisters of Jesus?

Q. My question is regarding Mary and Joseph. Are there actually any Bible verses that say Joseph was previously married or had children before he married Mary?

A. No Scripture says that Joseph had children before Mary, but we can come to that conclusion through some very simple detective work. For instance, the Bible tells us in several places that Jesus had brothers and sisters (see Matthew 12:46–50; 27:56; Mark 6:3; 16:1; Galatians 1:19). When Jesus was dying on the cross, He committed the care of His mother to the apostle John (John 19:25–27). That would have been a very unusual act if the other children had been her offspring. She would have automatically been under their care if that were the case.

Furthermore, during the time of Jesus, it was the duty of the oldest son in a family to stay home and work with the father to eventually take over his business. If Jesus had been the eldest, it would have been an insult to leave Joseph in the carpenter shop and go off preaching. But because Jesus was one of the younger sons, it wasn't a problem.

When we put these things together, it makes sense that Jesus was not Joseph's firstborn son. You typically hear about Mary and Joseph and Jesus' brothers and sisters. However, Joseph had died by the time Christ began His ministry, so scholars conclude that he was a little older than Mary and had already had a family before marrying her. His first wife had evidently passed away, and Joseph himself is never mentioned as being alive when Christ began His ministry.

A lot of this comes from mere deduction. Joseph died from old age and/or hard work by the time Jesus began His ministry. The older brothers of Christ continued working in the carpenter shop in Nazareth, and Jesus was Mary's only biological son. It cannot be proven from an exact Scripture, but most scholars accept this conclusion.

Why Did Moses and Elijah Appear?

If the dead do not go directly to heaven, then why did Moses and Elijah appear to Christ on the mount of transfiguration?

It's interesting that the last thing the Old Testament says is "Remember ye the law of Moses my servant, … Behold, I will send you Elijah the prophet" (Malachi 4:4, 5) Then in Matthew 17:3 and Mark 9:4, the two appear to Jesus and the disciples.

Jude 1:9 suggests that Michael, the archangel, resurrected Moses: "Michael the archangel, when contending with the devil he disputed about the body of Moses."

Jewish tradition says that three days after Moses died, the Lord came and resurrected him. We also have the example where Enoch was taken to heaven without dying (Genesis 22–24; Hebrews 11:5).

And then there was a special resurrection when Jesus died on the cross. Matthew 27:52, 53 says, "And the graves were opened; and many bodies of the saints which slept arose, And came out of the graves after his resurrection, and went into the holy city, and appeared unto many." But that was not a universal resurrection.

So there are some special exceptions of saved people from this life who are in glory now. But generally speaking, the mass exodus is going to be when the Lord descends from heaven.

The Egyptians of the Bible

 Are the Egyptians in the Bible the same people who built the pyramids?

Several different races have ruled the land we call Egypt. During the time of Joseph, a people ruled Egypt who allowed a Hebrew to co-rule with them. By Moses' lifetime, the people ruling Egypt were separationists who would not have knowingly allowed a Hebrew to rule with them. These, by the way, were the Egyptians who built the pyramids.

Control over Egypt has switched hands several times so that the country is actually a melting pot of many different races. The area has, at various times in history, been under the control of Babylonian, Persian, Greek, Roman, Turkish, French, British, and Israeli forces. Those who rule and live in Egypt today are a completely different people from those who built the pyramids. They are principally an Arabic people, descendants of Abraham's first son, Ishmael.

A Servant of the True God

 Who was Melchizedek?

Melchizedek is a king/priest who appears briefly in Genesis 14:18–20. Abraham was on his way back from a war with the kings of the north when he stopped to give tithe to the king of Salem. Although the Bible doesn't tell us much about him, we know that Melchizedek was a servant of the true God. The city of Salem later was known as Jerusalem.

In the New Testament, Paul tells us that Melchizedek is a symbol for Christ, because he suddenly appears on the scene and then he disappears. There's no lineage to tell us where he came from; this is like Christ, who is without beginning or end and who is our High Priest and King of the New Jerusalem.

Did Jephthah Sacrifice His Daughter?

 Did Jepthah put his daughter on an altar and kill her, as Judges 11:30–40 suggests?

Jephthah vowed that whatever first came out to meet him upon his return from a victorious battle, he would offer as a burnt offering (verse 31). When his daughter was the first to greet him, Jephthah said to her, "Thou hast brought me very low, and thou art one of them that trouble me: for I have opened my mouth unto the LORD, and I cannot go back" (verse 35). She answered, "My father, if thou hast opened thy mouth unto the LORD, do to me according to that which hath proceeded out of thy mouth; forasmuch as the LORD hath taken vengeance for thee of thine enemies, even of the children of Ammon" (verse 36).

The chapter goes on to say that he "did with her according to his vow which he had vowed" (verse 39). Notice, however, what she said in verse 37: "Let this thing be done for me: let me alone two months, that I may go up and down upon the mountains, and bewail my virginity." She was not bewailing her death, but her virginity.

I believe that what Jephthah did to fulfill his vow was similar to what Hannah did with Samuel (1 Samuel 1:27, 28). He brought his daughter to the sanctuary, and she was consecrated to the service of the Lord, which meant she was to remain celibate.

There are several biblical reasons why I believe Jephthah did not kill his daughter, but consecrated her instead.

First, human sacrifices were an abomination to Jehovah (Leviticus 18:21; 20:1–3; Jeremiah 32:35). We are told in Judges 11:29 that "The spirit of the LORD came upon Jephthah." Do you think that with the Spirit of the Lord upon him, he would have executed his daughter?

Second, Jephthah had it in his power to redeem his daughter. Leviticus 27:2 says, "Speak unto the children of Israel, and say unto them, When a man shall make a singular vow, the persons shall be for the LORD by thy estimation." In other words, if your firstborn was consecrated to the Lord, you weren't supposed to offer him as a sacrifice; you were to pay a price or offer an animal in his place.

Furthermore, only a priest was allowed to make a burnt offering (Leviticus 17:1–9). Remember how Saul got into trouble when he tried to assume the prerogative of a priest (1 Samuel 13:6–14)? What priest would have been willing to offer Jephthah's daughter, knowing this was an abomination to God?

Finally, the Bible says she bewailed her virginity, that she knew no man, and that the Israelite women went yearly to lament, or to comfort, her (Judges 11:38–40). Where did they go? They went to the temple, because her life was consecrated to the Lord.

Perhaps you are thinking, "Well, God asked Abraham to kill his son." True, but also remember that God stopped Abraham from doing it. Abraham did not kill Isaac, his son; God prevented him from carrying out His command. If Jephthah was led to victory by the Lord and willing to fulfill his vow, don't you think God would have stopped him before he shed his only child's blood?

I think it's clear what happened. Jephthah consecrated his daughter to the service of the sanctuary.

Will You Be With Me Today?

Q. My husband read in 1 Thessalonians that Christ's second coming will take place when He takes to heaven those who are dead, along with His children who are still alive. However, Christ told the robber on the cross that He would see him "today" in heaven. To what is the writer of 1 Thessalonians referring?

A. What your husband read in 1 Thessalonians 4:16, 17 is correct. Many have been confused about what Jesus was saying to the thief on the cross, as recorded in Luke 23:43. The way the comma was placed by translators, the sentence reads, "Assuredly, I say to you, today you will be with Me in Paradise" (NKJV). However, Jesus couldn't have meant that He would actually see the thief that day because He did not go to heaven that day. We know this because when we read the story in the Gospel of John, Mary goes to the tomb two days after Jesus died. When Jesus appears to Mary, she joyfully reaches out to Him, but He stops her. "Touch me not," He tells her, "for I am not yet ascended to my Father" (John 20:17).

What Jesus said was: "Assuredly, I say to you today, you will be with Me in Paradise." By misplacing a comma, the translator accidentally obscured what Jesus was telling the thief.

What Is the Origin of the Shroud of Turin?

 Do you think that the Shroud of Turin is real?

I personally don't believe that the Shroud of Turin is the actual burial cloth of Jesus. The Bible says that His body was bound in strips of linen with spices (John 19:40) and that a separate napkin was wrapped around His head (John 20:5–7). The Shroud of Turin, on the other hand, is a single cloth that was folded up the back and around the face of the body.

A few years ago when scientists began to do tests on the relic, evidence suggested that it did date back to the time of Christ and that it originated in Palestine. For example, they found pollen particles on it that were native only to Palestine. Later, researchers announced that the cloth dated back only to about A.D. 1300.

The Shroud of Turin may have been the result of a separate crucifixion. For example, Muslims punished some of the Crusaders by crucifying them just as the Romans crucified Jesus. As shocking as it may seem, there were also people during the Dark Ages who asked to be crucified in hopes that they would gain merit by experiencing the same torture and suffering that Jesus did. The Shroud of Turin could have been the grave cloth of someone in the Dark Ages who wanted to duplicate the sufferings of Christ. That would explain why it is stained with real blood and why there are so many similarities between the wounds imprinted on the cloth and those connected with a crucifixion.

Was Samuel's Risen Spirit Real?

 Explain how Samuel's spirit appeared to Saul in 1 Samuel 28.

"Then Saul said unto his servants, Seek me a woman that hath a familiar spirit, that I may go to her, and enquire of her. And his servants said to him, Behold, there is a woman that hath a familiar spirit at Endor" (1 Samuel 28:7).

King Saul went to a witch for advice! He didn't actually see Samuel, but rather a demon impersonating Samuel. There are several reasons we know that this was an evil deception. God said to never go to a witch. They were supposed to be executed. This "spirit" who came up and claimed to be Samuel said that the witch had the power to raise him. The Bible tells us that only God has the power to restore life and raise people from the dead. Jesus is the Resurrection and the Life. The devil can't give life to people.

The message that this spirit who claimed to be Samuel gave was an utterly hopeless, discouraging message. When Jesus gave people messages, He always mingled them with hope. If you read the seven messages to the seven churches in Revelation 2 and 3, He rebuked them, but He always said, "to him that overcomes." He mingled even the harshest messages with hope and mercy.

Part of the message this demon gave was, "To morrow shalt thou and thy sons be with me" (verse 19). The Bible tells us that Saul seems to have grieved away the Spirit, and an evil spirit took possession of him. He took his own life, and during the closing chapters of his life, God would not speak with him. That's why he went to the witch in the first place. So Saul died lost. Samuel died saved—a holy man, spirit-filled, prophet, and high priest. How could they possibly end up in the same place? It sounded like they were going to be sharing the same reward. So you see, there are so many suspicious things about the incident.

Saul ventured on the enchanted ground of that witch, and he was exposed to a demon who impersonated Samuel. Satan himself can be transformed into an angel of light (2 Corinthians 11:14). The devil has the power to create masterful illusions. This "appearance" of Samuel's spirit was one of those illusions.

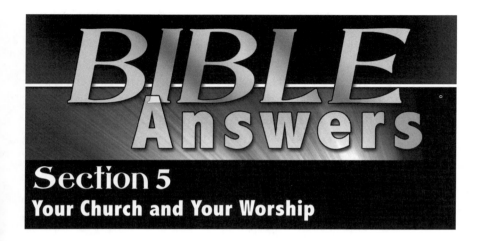

Going to Church

Q. Can a person find favor with God by living biblically but not going to church?

A. First, it's important to note that there will be many people in heaven who were not affiliated with a church, either because they did not have that opportunity or another reason that prevents them from that privilege. But one of the most important principles of Christianity is that we are saved into the body of Christ, which is another name for the church. In Acts 2, the Bible says, "And the Lord added to the church daily such as should be saved." When you are baptized, you become part of Christ's body and enter into the church.

I would also ask this question in return: Why would a person say they love God and His truth, but they don't wish to fellowship in love with His people? That's one of the reasons God wants us in church—because it has people with similar faith and beliefs. It helps bolster our faith and makes us accountable to one another. It is also an excellent environment to increase our capacity to love one another. People learn their most important lessons of love in the context of their biological families, and church families follow the same dynamic— especially when it comes to new believers. It is certainly a part of God's plan. If a person says, "I believe in God and the Bible and want to be saved and baptized, but I don't want to go to church," it sounds to me like a man saying to his bride, "I love you, I want to marry you—but I don't want to live with you." It's saying you want the benefits of marriage, but not the relationship that goes with it. Part of the Christian experience is having a relationship with the church—the fellowship of believers.

I lived as a hermit once—up in a cave and away from society. In that kind of solitude, you have a tendency to become eccentric. Isolating oneself from society and lacking social contact begin to affect your mind; your brain sort of atrophies. You become socially inept. In the same way, it's important for Christians to be social with fellow believers in corporate worship and gatherings to avoid becoming spiritually eccentric and inept. It's part of God's gift—so I encourage each Christian to find a biblical church in which they can grow into mature members of God's family.

The Music in Church

 Does the Bible say anything about the type of music we play or instruments we use in church?

This is a good and a big question because it addresses a very sensitive issue—where to draw the line in church music. In this short section, I can only touch on it. First, I've worshiped with conservative brethren who don't use any instruments in church. They have beautiful voices because they sing and harmonize without instruments. That's fine, and I believe the Lord has no problem with this. But I don't agree that it's wrong for Christians to use instruments in church. King David played harps in his praising the Lord. We'll even be playing them in heaven. They also played instruments in the sanctuary at God's instruction (2 Samuel 6:5).

I think you should consider two things when finding balance: the music and the lyrics. Both need to be something God can bless. Some Christian groups sing beautiful, profound lyrics—but the music sounds like a car crash. Sometimes you can't even tell what they're saying! Then you've got the other extreme: reverent music but with repetitive or unbiblical words. That's no better.

The music should be something that elevates our appreciation and understanding for the Lord. That's the kind of music that God will sanction, especially in His house of worship. It should be worshipful and convey a sense of reverence and love. It shouldn't be appealing to our lower natures with heavy syncopated rhythms that encourage dance fever. We all have a fleshly nature that music can bring about baser things in us; science affirms this!

I used to attend rock concerts, and you could easily see what the music did to the people. So you have to ask if the music is enhancing the words and lifting our souls heavenward or is it bringing out the animalistic sides of our natures. Jesus said, "You'll know them by their fruits."

A Joyful Noise?

 Is there anything wrong with jumping and clapping in church?

The Bible tells us that all things should be done "decently and in order" (1 Corinthians 14:40). You have to ask yourself, "What would Jesus do? What would the angels do?" If you can't picture Jesus jumping up and down in church, then I would question whether it was God's Spirit prompting someone to do it.

I can picture Christians rejoicing. I think the Jews rejoiced as Jesus rode down the hill on the donkey, and they shouted "hosanna." There is a time and place for rejoicing and clapping, but I don't think it is in the sanctuary during formal worship. If the music is taking control of us, then it may not be the appropriate music.

There is sometimes a very thin line between the music of rejoicing and the music of the world. We have to be very careful. I've seen a lot of churches in which that line is crossed, in my opinion.

When in doubt, do the safe thing. If you're questioning whether or not a certain activity is appropriate for glorifying God, then don't do it.

Confess to Our Brethren?

 Must we confess our sins to our Christian brethren to be forgiven?

Principally, all sin in general is against God and must be confessed only to Him in the closet of prayer. Notice that even after David sinned with Bathsheba and killed Uriah, he prayed, "Against thee, thee only, have I sinned, and done this evil in thy sight" (Psalm 51:4).

When Achan was identified by God for stealing, his sin was against God and the people. Joshua told him; "My son, I beg you, give glory to the LORD God of Israel, and make confession to Him, and tell me now what you have done; do not hide it from me" (Joshua 7:19). Because his sin directly affected the people, or church, he was commanded to acknowledge this publicly. But the confession was to God, not man—because only God can forgive sin. "I, even I, am He who blots out your transgressions for My own sake; And I will not remember your sins" (Isaiah 43:25).

But if we hurt, offend, or abuse another human whether Christian or pagan, we should acknowledge it and ask them to forgive us. "Therefore if you bring your gift to the altar, and there remember that your brother has something against you, leave your gift there before the altar, and go your way. First be reconciled to your brother, and then come and offer your gift" (Matthew 5:23, 24).

The simple rule is this: Public sin should be acknowledged publicly; offences against individuals should be addressed only with those involved. And private sin should be confessed to God in private.

Private Baptism?

 Is private baptism without a pastor biblically valid?

The people who baptized in Bible times were men who had been commissioned by God and given authority: the prophets, John the Baptist, and the apostles, for example. The Bible seems to establish this as a precedent.

Acts 6:3 says that when the apostles set up the office of deacon, they chose seven men who were "of honest report" and "full of the Holy Ghost and wisdom." Then, to make it official, these men were set before the apostles, who prayed and laid hands on them (verse 6). When Philip baptized the Ethiopian eunuch (Acts 8:26–39), we don't know if he was still a deacon or if he had been "promoted." We do know, however, that there is no record in the Bible of the disciples baptizing one another.

Let me tell you why I think that is. I'm a pastor, and if all of my church members believed they could go out and baptize whomever they felt led to baptize, without any kind of clearing process, they could wind up bringing people into the church who had not really been taught. Jesus said, "Go ye therefore, and teach all nations, baptizing them in the name of the Father, and of the Son, and of the Holy Ghost: Teaching them to observe all things whatsoever I have commanded you" (Matthew 28:19, 20, emphasis added).

I'm not going to make a dogmatic statement and say that God would not honor a private baptism at which no pastor is present. There have been Christians in Communist countries that accepted Jesus and then baptized each other. But they were operating under extreme circumstances.

If you do have Bible-teaching, Bible-believing churches in your community that teach and practice baptism by immersion, why wouldn't you want to participate in a public baptism and invite your pastor?

Closed Communion?

Q. Is communion only for those who are members of a particular church and those with their sins forgiven?

A. In 2 Corinthians 13:5, Paul says that every person should examine him or herself. He says, "Examine yourselves, whether ye be in the faith; prove your own selves." Notice that he doesn't say, "Examine each other." So I should not examine you, and you should not examine me. With that in mind, who can judge who should receive communion but each individual for themselves?

However, Jesus allowed Judas to participate in the communion even though He knew that Judas was stealing and about to betray Him. He did not forbid him despite these sins. As a matter of fact, Christ even washed his feet. So the communion should be redemptive in nature. Yet the Bible does say that we should not eat the bread or drink the blood to our own condemnation—the principle being that we have an unforgiving spirit (Matthew 5:23). Jesus said that if you bring a gift to the altar, and the communion is like a symbol of this, and you are angry with your brother, you are to leave your gift, be reconciled to your brother, and then offer your gift. So when we accept the sacrifice of Jesus, we should have a forgiving spirit in our hearts. But nobody should be in the church judging whether or not we are worthy to participate.

It's a very common human characteristic that we look at the problems that we see on the outside, and we don't recognize the hurt that's on the inside. When people come to communion, they're looking for cleansing, forgiveness, and healing and we need to allow that miracle to transpire.

I pastor at a church that practices what is called open communion. This means we allow individuals to judge themselves, and we do not police the hearts of our members and guests. Remember that Jesus is the example we must follow, and He did not decide who should and should not. So I think a church is more biblical if they practice open communion.

Christmas and Easter Displays

 My church displays a nativity for Christmas and a cross for Easter. Is that right?

I get a lot of these questions before and after both Easter and Christmas, and it's something to honestly consider. If your church is promoting these kinds of activities, choose your battles cautiously and be careful to not "major in minors."

Biblically, there is no command for us to worship the figure of the cross; but the principle of the cross is something

Christians should cherish even though the world despises it. But the Bible never even asks us to make crosses and carry them around as symbols. There is no record that the disciples did this either. In fact, the cross probably didn't become a prominent Christian "logo" until about 400 years after Christ, and the fish image was used more for identification in times of persecution.

Yet the cross has become the major symbol of Christianity. I don't make a big issue over it being used as a figurative emblem, so to speak, to identify the faith. But we are not to worship it. Nor are we to wear it as jewelry; instead we are commanded to bear the cross, which is a whole different concept. I think many put up crosses in their churches and around their necks because they don't want to truly bear it. If we would just bear the cross as Christ asks us, we wouldn't need to have all these external symbols.

And as for nativities, well, first of all, most of them are simply inaccurate. They usually show the shepherds and the wise men together at the manger. However, in the Bible, the wise men came into the house (Matthew 2:11) to worship Jesus. The shepherds and the wise men probably never saw each other, at least, not at the stable. Their visits were also probably a year apart.

However, if someone wants to portray a scene that helps young people and others to visualize and remember the sacrifice of Christ, I believe that's okay as long as we remember the second commandment: "Thou shalt not bow down thyself to them" (Exodus 20:5). It's still very important to remember that there is no mandate in the Bible to have a nativity, or even celebrate Jesus' birth. But if somebody wants to keep a day unto the Lord, let him or her keep it unto the Lord (Romans 14:6). So if people were going to celebrate the day of Christ's birth, then I would let them. Of course, Christ was not born on December 25— we're not sure exactly when He was born—but many people regard that day with sincerity. And as long as they are honoring that day unto the Lord, and not VISA or MasterCard or unto popular or pagan traditions, I think we should remember to keep the main thing the main thing.

A Rebuilt Temple

 Does the temple need to be rebuilt before Jesus returns?

In the same way that the devil has misdirected our focus from spiritual Israel to the literal headlines and events revolving around the Jewish nation today, he has also confused people on the subject of the temple.

Most of the speculation and hopes for a rebuilt temple spring from a vague reference in 2 Thessalonians 2 dealing with the Antichrist power. "Let no man deceive you by any means: for that day shall not come, except there come a falling away first, and that man of sin be revealed, the son of perdition; Who opposeth and exalteth himself above all that is called God, or that is worshiped; so that he as God sitteth in the temple of God, showing himself that he is God" (verses 3, 4). Many say that for the Antichrist to sit in the temple, it will obviously have to be rebuilt.

Those who support this belief are known as Christian Zionists, and they include such popular writers as Grant Jeffrey, Hal Lindsey, Tim LaHaye, and John Hagee, whose combined published book sales exceed 70 million in more than 50 languages—including the popular *Left Behind* series. Their beliefs are endorsed by some of the largest theological colleges and institutions as well as a significant portion of evangelical, Charismatic, Pentecostal, and fundamentalist Christians worldwide.

However, even a brief and hurried study of Scriptures will show the error behind this notion. To begin, we can go to 1 Chronicles 17:11, 12 to a dual prophecy concerning the temple. "And it shall come to pass ... that I will raise up thy seed after thee, which shall be of thy sons; and I will establish his kingdom. He shall built me an house, and I sill stablish his throne for ever." This is a prophecy given to King David, which clearly says his offspring will rebuild the temple. Later, in 1 Chronicles 28:6, God reaffirms to David, "Solomon thy son, he shall build my house and my courts."

This is one of the clearest examples of a dual prophecy found in Scripture. Dual prophecies in the Bible have both a physical and spiritual fulfillment. Indeed, Solomon was the son of David and he built the physical temple. But this prophecy also applies spiritually to Jesus, the true "Son of David," who was to build a temple and kingdom that was to last forever.

Jesus' prophecy that the pride of the Jewish nation, the temple, would be destroyed inspired the most intense rejection of His teaching. "And Jesus went out, and departed from the temple: and his disciples came to him for to show him the buildings of the temple. And Jesus said unto them, See ye not all these things? Verily I say unto you, There shall not be left here one stone upon another, that shall not be thrown down" (Matthew 24:1, 2).

And in Mark 14:58, Jesus says, "I will destroy this temple that is made with hands, and within three days I will build another made without hands." Of course, Jesus is making it very clear He is speaking of rebuilding a temple not out of stone and nails, but of living stones (1 Peter 2:5). Yet many refused to grasp this idea. "Then said the Jews, Forty and six years was this temple in building, and wilt thou rear it up in three days? But he spake of the temple of his body" (John 2:19–21). Their blindness to this clear explanation was used to mock Jesus as He hung on the cross. "Thou that destroyest the temple, and buildest it in three days, save thyself. If thou be the Son of God, come down from the cross" (Matthew 27:40). When Jesus died, the veil of the physical temple ripped in two from the top to bottom, signifying that the earthly temple no longer held meaning. A temple for sacrifice today would be as useless as it was then, and it would not be the house of God.

The New Testament is replete with the idea that the temple is the body of Jesus Himself. The next few Scriptures bear this out: Ephesians 2:19–22 says, "Now therefore ye are no more strangers and foreigners, but fellowcitizens with the saints, and of the household of God: and are built upon the foundation of the apostles and prophets; Jesus Christ himself being the chief corner stone; In whom all the building fitly framed together growth unto an holy temple in the Lord: In whom ye also are builded together for an habitation of God through the Spirit." This is later affirmed by 1 Peter 2:5, which says, "Ye also, as lively stones, are built up a spiritual house, an holy priesthood, to offer up spiritual sacrifices, acceptable to God by Jesus Christ."

Sadly, even after God provides all this clear biblical evidence that His temple today is a spiritual one, many Christians are waiting for the Jews to receive a construction permit to rebuild a physical temple on site where a Muslim mosque now sits. However, there is no prophecy, promise, or commandment in the Bible that says the physical temple would be rebuilt after the Romans last razed it.

Jewish Festivals

Should Christians take part in the Jewish festivals?

In 1 Corinthians 5:7, 8, Paul says, "Purge out therefore the old leaven, that ye may be a new lump. ... For even Christ our Passover is sacrificed for us: Therefore let us keep the feast, not with old leaven, neither with the leaven

of malice and wickedness; but with the unleavened bread of sincerity and truth." So Christ is our Passover; we no longer need to sacrifice a Passover lamb; Jesus is that Lamb. This same principal applies to the other Jewish festivals and feasts.

I have no burden to challenge those who feel convicted to observe these days, but I also don't see the point. I see no reason to keep the Jewish holidays that were a shadow of what Jesus was to do here on earth. Why embrace His shadow when He's before you in flesh and blood? Why stare at a loved one's photo when they're standing before you? Some feasts required worshipers to offer sacrifices at the Jerusalem temple, so it's obviously not possible to keep them now.

The festivals remembering the Exodus and the sanctuary were nailed to the cross when Jesus died (Colossians 2:16). They were shadows: the handwriting of ordinances on paper. To contrast, the unchanging Sabbath was written in stone. That is why the veil was ripped from top to bottom in Matthew 27:51. No man could have ripped that veil in that fashion; a clear indication from God that the types and shadows that pointed to Jesus ended with the crucifixion. And Daniel 9:27 prophecies this when it says, "And he shall confirm the covenant with many for one week: and in the midst of the week he shall cause the sacrifice and the oblation to cease." There were no Jewish holidays or feasts prior to the Exodus, and these were done away with when Christ completed His mission.

Bible Studies

 What's the best way to conduct a Bible study for a small group?

I think you can conduct Bible studies in numerous ways, depending on your personality and the desires and needs of the group.

A lot of people like to pick a specific chapter or book of the Bible and have the group read the passages. Then they can go back and read the verses again, pausing after each verse to discuss what it means to the group. If you run into something that you don't understand, look it up in the concordance and read cross-reference texts that shine light on it.

You could also take various characters from the Bible and study their traits, their habits, and their lives. This always makes for a fascinating study. Another approach is to use prepared Bible study materials.

I definitely believe that God's people should meet in houses around the world to study the Bible.

Repeating a Prayer

 Isn't praying for something once enough?

 Prayer is not merely informing God; it draws us up to God. It increases our intensity by wrapping us around God.

The Lord wants us to pray to Him for our benefit, not because He doesn't know what's going on. It binds us to God. The Lord lays certain burdens on our heart, and as long as those burdens are there, we should keep praying for them.

Prayer Repetition

 Where is the line between persisting in prayer and vain repetition?

Let's look at a couple of Bible answers. Jesus said, "When ye pray, use not vain repetitions, as the heathen do: for they think that they shall be heard for their much speaking. Be not ye therefore like unto them: for your Father knoweth what things ye have need of, before ye ask him" (Matthew 6:7, 8).

The heathen would utter the same prayer several times in one sitting. That's not prayer. Prayer is the intelligent cry of your heart to the heart of God. Prayer elevates you. When you pray, you should think about the prayer and what you're saying means.

There are even some professed Christian denominations that tell people that when they sin, they should say a certain prayer over and over again in order to right the wrong they did. That's not biblical. It's an insult to God, because He knows what you need before you ask.

Then you've got people like Elijah who knelt down and, seven times, asked God to send the rain. I don't think he prayed the exact same prayer seven times. Rather, seven different times he pled with the Lord to fulfill His Word and send the rain.

People who have children who are wandering from God pray for their salvation every day. That's not praying in vain repetition. You can bet that Jesus prayed for the apostles every day (John 17).

Worshiping an Image

Q. The Catholic Church seems to think that when we venerate an image, it is acceptable as long as we heed it as a reminder rather than actually worshiping the wooden statue. What do you think?

A. Ask any Buddhist, Hindu, or other person around the world who worships idols if they really think that statue is Buddha and they'll say: "No, of course not. It's there to help us visualize Buddha." So the argument Catholics use for bowing before statues is the very same argument used by every single pagan religion of the world. "We know that the statue isn't really this god," they'll say. "The image is there to help us visualize and to have more faith in that god."

That's still idolatry. The second commandment in God's eternal law says not to make images or to bow down before them (Exodus 20:4, 5). That's what the Bible says.

Women in the Pulpit

 What does the Bible say about women as church leaders or preachers?

God made men and women as equal creatures. I do not believe there is any distinction between men and women in their value to God and their accessibility to salvation. They're both perfectly equal.

Furthermore, God ministers through both men and women. You read in the Bible both about men and women teaching and preaching, in the capacity of prophets and evangelists, or giving Bible studies as did Priscilla with her husband, Aquila (Acts 18:26).

However, there is no example in the Bible of a woman serving in the capacity of priest, pastor, or elder.

When Jesus chose the 12 apostles, I do not believe He was accommodating the traditions of the day when He selected only men. Several offices have a uniquely male symbolism. For example, the men were to be the priests of their families. That means servant-leaders, not dictators or despots. Consider Moses' family. Amram and Jochebed had three children: Miriam, Aaron, and Moses. All three were prophets. Their sons both served as priests, but Miriam did not. She was a prophetess, but not a priest. She led the women in prophetic songs and in teaching.

You read about Anna in the temple (Luke 2:36, 37) and Deborah as a prophetess and a judge in Israel (Judges 4:4), but you never read of women offering a sacrifice. In the Bible, a priest is a male role because it symbolizes Jesus, our High Priest. A similar distinction was made for the Passover sacrifice. The Israelites were instructed to take a male lamb because it was a symbol for Christ.

God has distinctions in the family and in roles within the family. I don't think these sexual identities evaporate when people walk through the doors of the church. It is an extension of the individual family unit. There's a lot of Scripture to support this: Ephesians 5:23–25; 1 Timothy 2:12; Titus 1:6; and 1 Corinthians 11:3–16, for example.

"If a Woman is Not Covered..."

 Should women cover their heads in church?

Paul writes, "But every woman who prays or prophecies with her head uncovered dishonors her head. ... If a woman is not covered, let her also be shorn. But if it is shameful for a woman to be shorn or shaved, let her be covered" (1 Corinthians 11:5, 6).

The Bible also says that in the mouth of two or three witnesses, let a thing be established. We should be careful not to build a doctrine on one Scripture that might in fact stand by itself. This is the only place in the Bible where it talks about this particular issue. It appears at first glance Paul is insisting women who pray or prophecy in the church in public prayer and corporate worship—not in private—do so with their heads covered or veiled.

The argument is whether or not this is an out-dated tradition or something women must do today. In the Middle

East now especially, some Islamic women still dress like Bible women used to dress; they are very modest, maybe to a fault. In the days of the Roman Empire, the time in which Paul writes, a woman would cover her head because it was one way to avoid being thought a prostitute, who would go around with her head uncovered as part of her provocative attire.

Adam Clark, in his Bible commentary, shares some interesting thoughts; "It was a custom, both among the Greeks and Romans, and among the Jews an express law, that no woman should be seen abroad without a veil. This was, and is, a common custom through all the east, and none but public prostitutes go without veils. And if a woman should appear in public without a veil, she would dishonor her head—her husband. And she must appear like to those women who had their hair shorn off as the punishment of whoredom, or adultery." In the Bible, we find this was a practice for women suspected of adultery. "Then the priest shall set the woman before the LORD, [and] uncover the woman's head" (Numbers 5:18).

Some wonder if this was simply a tradition, and Paul was asking women to honor that tradition out of respect. You can compare this to a President who gives a national address and doesn't wear a tie. Many believe that isn't appropriate. But nothing in the Constitution, and much less the Bible, says he must wear a tie. There's not even a good practical reason—I don't like them one bit! But it's a custom of respect of which the President should be mindful.

Likewise, in the ancient churches, evidently they thought it was disrespectful for Christian women to pray or prophesy in public with their husbands present and with their heads uncovered. It was considered immodest, and they didn't show modesty or respect for their husbands. So it was very likely just a simple tradition that Paul was encouraging the church to respect in order to improve the witness of the church among the culture of the day.

However, if the Holy Spirit is convicting a woman to cover her head as a sign of respect when praying in public, I have no burden to discourage her from doing so. There is certainly no harm in covering your head during prayer. But if you're in doubt, remember that Paul said if you can't do something by faith, don't do it. "For whatsoever is not of faith is sin" (Romans 14:23).

And be careful not to judge in your heart or with words those who are not under the same conviction.

Balancing Unity with Doctrine

Q. What is the balance between church unity and sound doctrine? Also, what would you consider the bare minimum a person must know about Christ and the gospel to be saved?

A. There is a real push lately calling Christians to lay aside their differences and just unite for the purposes of serving society. I think there are areas where we can cooperate, but I don't think we should ever sacrifice principles of essential truth.

What are these principles? We need to know first what sin is. That's not where everyone would start, but the Bible tells us that the first thing about knowing whether you're saved is knowing that you're lost. We must understand that sin is the transgression of God's law, and that Jesus came to save us from our sins, from our disobedience. We need to believe that we are saved by grace through faith. And we need to know that He not only pardons the sins in our past, but He gives us power to live a new victorious life, a life of overcoming sin, representing Him, and being spirit-filled. These are just a few of the basics of Christian faith.

Renew Your Devotion

 What's the best way to renew your mind when you've fallen away?

The crucial thing you must do is maintain a regular daily devotional life. In order to become, and remain, close to God, you need to read your Bible and pray every day. Don't lose the habit of regularly feeding your soul on the Word of God. The Bible says, "Thy word have I hid in mine heart, that I might not sin against thee" (Psalm 119:11).

If you're struggling with any sort of temptation, you need more of God's Spirit—more of Christ—in you and He's the living Word. As you read the Word, Jesus comes into your heart and mind, and that's what keeps you from sinning. If you fill your life with the light of Christ, it crowds the darkness of the devil away.

Bible Truth in Church

How do you determine your opinion from the facts? What's the difference between Bible-believing churches and off-the-wall cults?

The answer to this is really quite simple. When comparing Scriptures to one another, you'll see the picture God wants you to see. It's like putting a puzzle together piece by piece. If you have to jam pieces into place, you're doing something wrong. They should fit easily together; there's searching involved, but you shouldn't have to force the text. We must let the Bible interpret itself.

So Bible-believing churches should base their conclusions on what the Bible says, without allowing an individual or group to interpret everything for its members. Several members should study the Bible and bounce ideas off one another. The Bible says, "In the multitude of counselors there is safety."

Cults are classified as such because an elite person or inner circle does all the thinking for the followers—when members disagree they can't challenge or take a stand against them. People blindly following this kind of practice without Bible study are in danger of being lost!

A cult also forbids members from looking at outside literature. Some come knocking on my door wanting to study the Bible with me. They are almost always sincere, and I admire their enthusiasm. But before they leave, I offer them a book. Yet they won't dare take it, because their church is afraid that their doctrines won't stand up under scrutiny. A challenge to the church is forbidden.

The Bible says, "Try the spirits and hold fast to that which is good." We ought to prove all things. So we need to keep our eyes open. You don't need to look at garbage, but you must examine and evaluate truth, holding fast to the good. With heartfelt prayer and study, God will lead you.

Are There Biblical Principles on Dating?

Q. What does the Bible have to say about dating and choosing a life partner? What about holding hands and kissing?

A. When dating, I think most of us know some very basic principles. Simply socializing with another Christian is very different than choosing a life partner. When mingling with other members of the faith, ensure you're in a Christian environment that is spiritually edifying.

And when it comes to choosing a potential partner for life, you don't want to be unequally yoked. Being compatible, both emotionally and spiritually, is important. It is best to avoid the trappings of worldly dating that consists largely of hugging and kissing simply to see if you've got chemistry. Though the Bible does say to greet each other with a brotherly kiss, it's talking about something very different. When Jacob kissed Rachel, it was a greeting—a peck on the cheek is much different than the kissing that turns into forbidden foreplay and fornication.

I'm kind of old-fashioned, and I think that when two people are courting they are better off having little physical contact. I think holding hands and a farewell kiss on the cheek is probably plenty. When you start fooling with nature, it can get carried away very quickly. Don't fool with temptation. People don't have to share a bed to find out if they're compatible.

I tell young couples that if they want to determine if they can get along, they should try sharing a checkbook or go shopping together. These will say a lot about a potential partner. Also, if you want to know them better, find out what their values are and what they read. Also watch how they treat their parents, because that's how they are going to treat you. These are the things that really matter.

Sons of God Marrying the Daughters of Man?

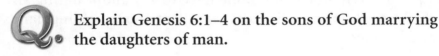

Q. Explain Genesis 6:1–4 on the sons of God marrying the daughters of man.

A. The Bible says: "And it came to pass, when men began to multiply on the face of the earth, and daughters were born unto them, That the sons of God saw the daughters of men that they were fair; and they took them wives of all which they chose. And the LORD said, My spirit shall not always strive with man, for that he also is flesh: yet his days shall be an hundred and twenty years. There were giants in the earth in those days; and also after that, when the sons of God came in unto the daughters of men, and they bare children to them, the same became mighty men which were of old, men of renown" (Genesis 6:1–4).

First, let's identify the "sons of God." There have been Bible paraphrases that say these "sons of God" are heavenly beings, or angels, that had intimate relations with human women. There's nothing in the Bible that suggests that angels procreate— with other angels or humans. These paraphrases are largely responsible for people's misunderstanding of this verse. If we let the Bible interpret itself, we see that these "sons of God" were not angels at all.

Look at the genealogy of Jesus in Luke 3:38, "Which was the son of Enos, which was the son of Seth, which was the son of Adam, which was the son of God." Adam was called the "son of God." Then flip over to 1 John 3:1, "Behold, What manner of love the Father hath bestowed upon us, that we should be called the sons of God." These two instances show us that "sons of God" are human people that are committed to the Lord.

After Cain killed Able, Adam and Eve had another son named Seth. Seth, it says, feared the Lord (Genesis 4:25, 26). Seth and his descendants were children of God. Cain was carnal, and he did not have everlasting life. As long as their descendants remained separate, the truth of God was preserved. But when the "sons of God," the descendants of Seth, began to intermarry with the wicked daughters of Cain, that distinction and holiness evaporated. That's why Genesis 6:3 says that God's spirit would not always be with man and that he had 120 years before the Flood.

What Does the Bible Say About Divorce?

Q. Explain why the adultery exception for divorce is only in Matthew and the meaning of sexual immorality.

A. There are several stories that appear in the gospels only once. For instance, only in Luke do you find the prodigal son, Zaccaeus, the 99 sheep, the Good Samaritan, and so forth. The Gospel writers wrote what the Holy Spirit really impressed on their lives, just like witnesses all record and testify to different aspects of one event.

As far as there not being other examples in the Bible of divorce exceptions, here's what I believe. Remember the thief on the cross who gave his heart to Jesus just hours before he died? In his commentary, Matthew Henry says, "The reason for this example is so none need lose hope. But the reason there is only one example is so that none would presume to wait until the eleventh hour." If Jesus had lots of loopholes in the gospel for divorce, by our natural evil bent, we would take advantage of that.

What About Heavenly Marriages?

Q. Will there be marriages in heaven?

A. There's only one reference in Scripture that alludes to this, Matthew 22:30. Jesus said to the Sadducees, "For in the resurrection they neither marry, nor are given in marriage, but are as the angels of God in heaven." Based on that Scripture, we have reason to believe there are going to be no new marriages in the kingdom.

We Don't Need Tithing in Today's World, Do We?

Q. The Bible says that if we pay tithe, "God will open up the windows of Heaven and we will not have room to receive it." Does that apply to us today or was that done away with?

A. The New Testament says comparatively little about tithe. But it does not condemn tithing or cancel it. Tithing is a system that God employed to support the ministry of His Word. When the Jews neglected tithing in the Old Testament, the people backslid because the priests were unable to teach—they were back on the farm again! Tithing was an important way to supply their needs so they could circulate throughout Israel and teach Scripture. The need is still there for ministers to be sustained by the tithe so that they can focus on teaching.

I'm a pastor, and I work all through the week—comforting the ill, praying with people, and preaching to the lost. If I had to work full time at another job, I could not minister as I do. So God also designed this system for today. Christ mentions tithing just once in reference to how the hypocrites pay their tithe, but omit weightier matters of the law and love. He says, "These they ought to have done and not leave the other undone." Do not leave tithing undone—that's a pretty clear statement from Jesus (Matthew 23:3).

Paul adds, "You should not muzzle the ox that treads the grain" (1 Timothy 5:18). And he appeals to the Old Testament laws in connection with tithing, even though he doesn't explicitly call it tithing. He says, "Those that preach the gospel should be sustained by the gospel." That was the Old Testament principle. He never says that tithing is nothing, unlike circumcision. We're to assume that it's still intact.

I believe that God still opens up the windows of heaven. When I first came to Jesus, everything I owned fit in a backpack. When I started paying tithe, even on my meager income, the Lord blessed my family! He's glorified me for honoring Him. I've seen countless miracles in the lives of people who claim those promises of tithing, and they're still available today. "Prove me now," says the Lord. Claim that promise, and He'll bless you.

Will I Retire Before Jesus Comes?

 If we believe Jesus is coming soon, is it a lack of faith for us to prepare for retirement?

A. Planning for retirement doesn't represent a lack of faith. I believe Christians should have a relationship with the Lord in which they remember that they could die or that Jesus could come at any time, yet plan for the future as though this earth could last for another hundred years.

Jesus told a parable in Luke 19:12–27 about a ruler who went away on a long trip but promised to return. Before he left, the man called 10 of his servants and gave them a very large sum of money. His parting instructions were "Do business till I come" (verse 13 NKJV). In other words, Jesus was telling His disciples to stay busy, invest, and plan for the future. Anything we do should be done as unto the Lord. This means we must do things to last.

For example, if you are going to build a house, don't build it to last only five years even if you believe the Lord is coming soon. My advice is to dig deep and build your foundation well. The Bible says, "Whatsoever your hand findeth to do, do it with thy might" (Ecclesiastes 9:10).

I once heard a story that helps to illustrate this point.

A young monk living in a monastery was reading some of the Scriptures chained to the wall that told about the eminence of Christ's coming. He got very excited and ran out to St. Francis, who was hoeing peas in the garden.

The young monk exclaimed, "Jesus is coming!"

"Yes, my son," St. Francis replied.

"He's coming soon," emphasized the young man.

Saint Francis acknowledged, "I know, my son."

"Well," asked the monk, "how can you just sit there and hoe your peas? What if He was going to be coming tomorrow? What would you be doing now?"

"Well, first I'd finish hoeing the peas," St. Francis answered.

That's the attitude I think Christians should have. Be faithful in what lies closest to you, because we don't know the day or the hour of Jesus' return (Mark 13:32–33).

Where Should My Inheritance Go?

Q. Is it proper for a Christian to leave an inheritance to unconverted children who might squander it selfishly?

A. Two facets must be considered when addressing this issue: love for God (loyalty to His cause) and unconditional love for your children.

It is important to communicate love to all our children in our estate planning. If the last act of a parent's life is to totally cut a son or daughter out of the will, an adult child might be forever turned from accepting the Lord. This leaves a bitter scar that is almost impossible for children to forget. "A good man leaveth an inheritance to his children's children" (Proverbs 13:22).

The other dynamic is that we must give an account to God for how we distribute our assets at the time of our deaths. To leave considerable wealth to unconverted children is, for practical purposes, placing God's resources, which could be used to save souls, in the devils hands. "He that loveth son or daughter more than me is not worthy of me" (Matthew 10:37).

The answer is balance. You might naturally want to leave enough for your children and grandchildren to communicate love and thoughtfulness or provide for practical needs such as education. Giving non-cash assets, such as property and family heirlooms, can also convey this.

Before David died, he told his son Solomon that he arranged to leave the bulk of his assets to build up God's house. "Indeed I have taken much trouble to prepare for the house of the LORD one hundred thousand talents of gold and one million talents of silver, and bronze and iron beyond measure, for it is so abundant" (1 Chronicles 22:14).

You can be sure that David left a generous inheritance for Solomon and all his children, but there is no doubt that the majority of his prosperity went to build up the House of God. This is an excellent example for Christian parents today.

Parents set a lasting example and make a powerful impression when their children see that they choose to seek first God's kingdom with their estate planning.

Entertainment Tonight?

 What is biblically permissible when it comes to entertainment?

The Bible says in Philippians 4:8, "Whatsoever things are pure, whatsoever things are lovely, whatsoever things are of good report ... think on these things."

If you apply these criteria to what you're watching, reading, and hearing, this is always the safest guide. Is your choice of entertainment elevating? Is it noble? Is it true? These are some of the tests that Paul applies regarding how we determine what to think about.

King David said, "I will set no wicked thing before mine eyes" (Psalm 101:3).

When we follow this as a guideline, we're more likely to choose activities that nurture the fruits of the spirit. And the bottom line is always, "What would Jesus do?" What would He watch, what would He read, and what would He listen to? These are very good questions to ask yourself in every situation. A Christian is a follower of Christ, so His example should be foremost in our minds and hearts. The only way to really find that out is to study your Bible.

And as a final caution, don't be deceived simply by things called "Christian" or "family" entertainment. For instance, the *Left Behind* books and films are not only filled with misleading errors, they have violent scenes outside biblical context.

You can also apply this to the trendy Christian rock scene and similarly to the popular Christian culture at large. There is a reason why much of these types of entertainments are on the rise, and I don't think God has very much to do with them.

Good Movies in Bad Theaters?

 Is it wrong for a Christian to attend the theater for a "good" movie?

I'll answer this important question with a scenario. You can buy orange juice, which is perfectly good and healthful, at a supermarket or a bar. Traditionally, a Christian would not want to buy their orange juice at a bar because: 1) the environment is not the best; 2) the influence to try something inappropriate is much stronger; 3) people seeing a Christian go into a bar don't know that they are going for orange juice; and 4) you're going to pay a lot more for your orange juice than you would in a supermarket.

I think you can see the application. Just as the bar serves more liquor than orange juice, the typical movie shown in the theater is rated R, and theaters are a place where the viewing of violence, sex, and using God's name in vain are far more prominent than the very rare "good" movie.

You're also going to pay a lot more money than if you wait to see the video. With a little patience and just a few dollars, the whole family can enjoy the occasional "good film" together at home. The theater cost might affect your ability to act with discernment as well. If you've paid all that money to get in to the movie, and then find out that it's offensive, you won't have as much will power to walk out. And you won't have the option of a fast forward, mute, or off button!

You need to consider the effect of your witness as well. I know that many people would get the wrong impression if they saw Pastor Doug standing in line at a theater! In a multi-complex theater, they wouldn't know whether I was going in to see one of the immoral, scandalous flicks, or something more innocent. Our influence on others can be immense, and 1 Thessalonians 5:22 tells us to "Abstain from all appearance of evil." We also find this good advice in Romans 14:13, 19: "Let us not therefore judge one another any more: but judge this rather, that no man put a stumblingblock or an occasion to fall in his brother's way. … Let us therefore follow after the things which make for peace, and things wherewith one may edify another."

The "Good Fun" of Halloween?

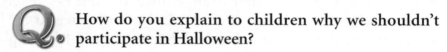

Q. How do you explain to children why we shouldn't participate in Halloween?

A. I have five children, so this question hits close to home. Two of the little Batchelor boys will have their noses pressed up against the window unless we take them to another program. Sometimes you can create a positive diversion. You don't have to be at your house. Most churches have some sort of harvest programs for children so they have a positive alternative to traditional Halloween antics. More than half the time, that's what happens in our family. Other times, you need to take them to the Bible and share with them from your heart. Tell them that sometimes Christians cannot participate in things that the world promotes as "good fun" if Jesus does not approve. Ask them to think about most of the costumes they see—dismembered humans, devils, ghosts, witches, and sometimes even politicians! Make sure they understand that it's something that makes Jesus unhappy, and that if they love Jesus, sometimes they'll have to say "no" to things that seem like harmless fun. You could also have your kids answer the door when someone knocks and hand out Bible lessons and that sort of thing.

Render to Caesar ... ?

Q. Is it appropriate for Christians to contribute to political campaigns?

A. First and foremost, in every Christian life there should be a priority to recognize that we are ambassadors of another kingdom and use the bulk of our sacrifice to spread the message of the gospel that we love. But there are a number of needs in the world and Christians should be known as givers not only to their cause, but also to various other causes in their society. This may mean helping with community projects of various kinds.

Although many politicians are not ethical, there are many who are. They are working to preserve the freedoms that mean so much to all of us. If an individual Christian feels convicted and inspired to contribute to a political issue that would expand the principles of Jesus, there is no moral dilemma in doing that. "Render to Caesar the things that are Caesar's, and to God the things that are God's" (Mark 12:17).

... That which is Caesar's?

Q. Please elaborate on the relationship between church and state.

A. No government can survive without supporting at least the last six of the Ten Commandments. It was no accident that God wrote the Ten Commandments on two tables of stone. Jewish tradition tells us that the Lord divided it this way: The first four, which deal with our relationship to God, are on the first table of stone, and the last six, which deal with our relationships with our fellow man, are on the second table of stone. I hear religious leaders talking about "America returning to God," and that we need to require that people keep the Ten Commandments. That scares me, because if the government dictates that we're supposed to keep the first four, they're going to tell us what God to worship, what day to worship Him, how to worship Him, what His name is, and so on. The government should never be involved in enforcing with civil penalties or laws the first four. But on the other hand, if the government does not endorse the last six, you have anarchy. That's where I draw the line. There is a misconception where people talk about Thomas Jefferson's reference to the wall of separation of church and state. He wasn't saying that religion and Christian principles should have no influence on government. He was saying that government should never dictate what the denomination of the state should be, which is what happened in Europe and in England. But the morals of Christianity and Judeo-Christian ethics must influence government, because they encompass the foundational morals that are essential for the survival of any society.

Gambling With Your Stewardship?

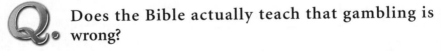 **Does the Bible actually teach that gambling is wrong?**

I believe the Bible does teach gambling is wrong. For one thing, we can save ourselves much confusion by applying a simple principle. A Christian is a follower of Jesus. God became a man to give us an everyday example. If you can picture Jesus in Vegas, yanking on a one-armed bandit, then it might be okay. But I have trouble conjuring up that picture.

Also, the atmosphere in gambling establishments is not very godly. Drinks are flowing, people aren't thinking about God; instead, they're thinking about worshiping money. Solomon says in Proverbs 23:4, "Do not overwork or do not strive to be rich." The reason people gamble is they want to get rich quick. The idea of gaining instant wealth without working is not really a biblical principle. The love of money is the root of all evil. Money is not evil, but the love of it.

Now if gambling in general is bad, then small degrees of gambling could also be a bad witness to others. You have a better chance of getting bit by a shark on dry land than winning the lottery in most states.

Are You Going to Get Lucky This Time?

 Does the Bible say Christians shouldn't play the lottery?

There is no direct Scripture about the lottery. The Bible says: "A faithful man shall abound with blessings: but he that maketh haste to be rich shall not be innocent. … He that hasteth to be rich hath an evil eye, and considereth not that poverty shall come upon him" (Proverbs 28:20, 22). People who play the lottery are trying to get money quickly without earning it. The thing that really worries me about this is the principle of stewardship. Many people who can barely rub two pennies together spend their last dollars on lottery tickets or in casinos. But the Bible command for Christians is to work and to eat from the labor of your hands (Genesis 3:19; Proverbs 14:23; Ephesians 4:28; 2 Thessalonians 3:12). Lotteries and gambling establishments prey on people's weaknesses, usually taking money from the poor who are sucked into a fantasy of wealth. Also, the lottery is one of the government's ways of getting welfare money back. God wants us to be faithful with the money He gives us. The Bible is very clear about that. A lot of people throw away thousands upon thousands of dollars thinking, "I'm going to get lucky this time."

Is the Stock Market Really Gambling?

 Is it a sin for Christians to invest in the stock market?

There is a way of working the stock market like a horse race—gambling, speculating, buying and selling on a day-by-day basis hoping that you'll make a profit, and then sell out. That's dangerous.

On the other hand, there are people who invest in legitimate businesses offering good products or services because they believe the business will see growth. Statistics show that if anyone invests in a solid and legitimate business, over the long haul the trend is always up. It seems better to invest than to leave your money in a bank.

Jesus tells us in the parable of the talents that we should invest for profit. We are to trade with the money He has given us. But I don't think Christians should be buying stock in alcohol, tobacco, drug companies or those that support abortion, produce deviant movies, and other things that aren't right.

When you put your money in the bank, you are indirectly investing in the stock market. If you're going to invest on your own, make sure you're putting your money in stocks that Jesus will approve.

Does God Approve of Slavery?

Q. How could a God of love make a statute in Leviticus 25 allowing slavery? Was slavery a curse against blacks? What does slavery say about God's character?

A. I don't believe it was ever God's plan for anybody to be or own slaves. We must remember that many of the ordinances in the Bible are meant to protect civilization and people from activities or customs of which God didn't approve.

For instance, there was rampant polygamy in Bible times. Part of the reason for this practice was that war was a way of life and there were 10 women for every man. Unfortunately, it was shameful for women to never have a family. Isaiah 4:1 it says that during those times, seven women would take hold of one man. Yet because polygamy is often discussed and apparently unpunished throughout the Bible, this doesn't mean it was God's will. In the same way, Jesus said divorce was not God's will, but He made that provision because of the hardness of men's hearts. He made these laws to protect the second wife—and he also made laws to protect slaves. He isn't endorsing slavery.

Some of the curses that you find in prophecy deal with nations warring with Israel. They never have a relationship to a race of people. There are prophetic curses against Ammonites, Edomites, Jebusites, Babylon—not races, but pagan nations at war with God's people. The Ethiopians were at war with Israel at different times in history, but Moses married an Ethiopian and an Ethiopian eunuch that converted to Christianity (Acts 7:8) brought Jesus to his country. Nothing in the Bible shows that God approves of segregation based on race. As a matter of fact, Acts tells us that God made all nations of one blood. You won't find support in the Bible for racism.

We also must understand, before we determine what a merciful God is all about, that slavery comes in different forms. The Word of God is the only thing that can set us free, so whether we are in slavery to another individual or to Satan or a sin, our freedom is based solely upon if we allow His Word to work within us. We can be locked up in prison, but we can still know freedom.

Some people walk through life imprisoned by the devil. But God allows what we will allow. He doesn't force anything on us. He tells us what we need to do to live a full, happy life, and we need to acknowledge that we can walk free. Otherwise, we'd be slaves to God. People too often focus on the little mysteries that puzzle them, oblivious to the glaring truth.

God hates slavery. There will be no slavery in heaven. There was no slavery before sin. God had certain laws to accommodate the hardness of humanity's heart that could allow such a vile practice.

Shoot to Kill?

Q. Should a police officer kill someone in the line of duty? The Bible says, "Thou shalt not kill" (Exodus 20:13).

A. The sixth commandment is literally translated as "Thou shalt not murder." God does not condemn killing for self-defense (Exodus 21:12, 13) or in cases of unintentional accident (Numbers 35:10, 11; 20–24; Deuteronomy 4:41, 42). In fact, there were times when God commanded His people to kill the enemies threatening their lives (Numbers 31:1–8; Deuteronomy 13:12–18). A police officer who is defending other people's lives as well as his own may sometimes have to use deadly force, and the Bible does not forbid this.

Righteous Anger?

 Is it OK to get angry with someone who sins against God (for example, someone who curses)?

When we hear those kinds of things, it's all right to disagree and to be upset with what was said. At the same time, we shouldn't be angry with the person who sinned. Many times people don't realize the seriousness of what they are doing. Even if someone does do it purposefully, we should follow Jesus' example. When Jesus was dying on the cross and people were blaspheming Him, He prayed, "Father, forgive them; for they know not what they do" (Luke 23:34). Jesus' attitude is the same one we should have toward people who curse Him.

Wars and Rumors of Wars?

The fear of wars and rumors of wars has plagued the world in recent years. Is this what Jesus is talking about when He speaks about wars and rumors of wars?

One of the signs of Jesus' second coming is that there would be major wars (Matthew 24:6). There certainly have been wars and rumors of wars in the last few years, most recently in the 9/11 terrorist attacks, Israel, and Indian and Pakistan. And in this century alone, hundreds of wars have cost more human life than in all the other previous centuries combined! These are certainly signs of the nearness of Christ's coming; but beyond that, the Bible is a book that talks about more than just battles between nations.

I once punched the word "war" into my Bible computer program while researching for a broadcast. I was amazed that the search found the word more than 200 times—not including the plural form! I believe the reason the Bible talks about battles so much is that they also act as object lessons that teach us how to overcome our own internal wars. The Bible is loaded with this kind of terminology. We're all fighting the good fight of faith, as Paul says in Timothy 1:28.

In 2 Timothy 2 he adds, "You therefore must endure hardship as a good soldier of Jesus Christ. No one engaged in warfare entangles themselves in the affairs of this life, that he might please him who enlisted him as a soldier."

Furthermore, 2 Corinthians 10:3–4 states, "For though we walk in the flesh, we do not war according to the flesh. For the weapons of our warfare are not carnal but mighty for pulling down strongholds."

That all ties into what Peter says. "Beloved, I beg you as sojourners and pilgrims to abstain from fleshly lusts that war against the soul" (1 Peter 2:11).

There is the war going on between the spirit and the flesh, between the Lord and the devil. The battleground is our minds and hearts. Some people say they are not going to worry about that; they'll just let the battle rage. There is danger if we do not resist the enemy; we can reach a point of no return by not defending our bodies and minds. The war of all wars is the struggle over a man's soul between Satan and Jesus. There is a great controversy being played out, and they're not fighting over geographic dirt. They are fighting over the allegiance of intelligent creatures in this world.

The character of God is at stake here. Many people are putting off deciding which side they are on, and this battle has placed them in deadly peril.

No Light in Secret Societies?

 What is the biblical principle to secret societies?

A. A secret society is a group that often meets in secret places closed to public viewing. Examples include elite organizations like the Mason society and even some religions.

Throughout the Bible, Jesus says we should walk in the light. When people are doing things in a dark place, it casts doubts. But Christians should be transparent and crystal clear, and shouldn't be taking secret oaths. Jesus says let our nays be nays, and our yeas be yeas—we shouldn't be swearing by things shrouded in secret. And so many policies and principles in secret societies contradict the clarity, honesty, and openness of Christianity.

In John 15:15, "Henceforth, I call you not servants, for the servant doesn't know what his lord is doing. But I have called you friends; for all the things I have heard of my father I have made known to you." Jesus is not keeping secrets; He is being open with us. Honestly, transparency, and openness—whatever you want to call them—should all be Christian characteristics.

BIBLE Answers

Section 7
Biblical Principles of Life and Death

Does Unclean Food Cancel Salvation?

Q. What about the people who eat unclean animals like pork, shrimp, lobster, etc? Will they go to heaven?

A. This question addresses those people who eat some of the animals that God calls unclean, and therefore unfit for human consumption, in the Bible. Is it a sin? Well, it depends on what the Lord has revealed to the person. If a person knows that God forbids these things, we know by example in the Bible that he or she should avoid eating them. For instance, in Daniel 1, the Babylonians offered Daniel a diet that included unclean foods. He said, "I cannot defile myself with a portion of the kings food." He would have died before he ate the Babylonian food because he knew better—it's really a question of loyalty; what will you do when you learn the truth? For certain, there will most likely be an uncountable number of believers in the kingdom who probably ate things that the Bible calls forbidden, because they don't know any better. This is why it tells us in Acts 17:30, "At the times of this ignorance, God winks at." When we don't know, God shows us mercy.

Sin is knowing to do good and not doing it; that's one of the Bible definitions for sin. When we know God's will and don't do it, that's a sin. And so whether it's the Sabbath or your body as a temple of the Holy Spirit, God wants us to live up to the light He gives us. If you know the truth but don't act on it, what does that tell God?

Can't We Now Eat Anything?

 What is the context in 1 Corinthians 10, when Paul appears to say eat anything that is sold in the meat market?

Well, first we have to ask the ridiculous question, which is: "Is the Lord saying you can eat anything?" I think we probably know the answer to that.

Even today, Jesus has warned us not to tempt the Lord, and modern medicine is very clear that there are some things you can eat and some food that is very bad for your health. The Bible says, "Don't be deceived, God is not mocked. Whatever a man sows, he'll also reap."

However, the context of 1 Corinthians 10 really has nothing to do with which meats are acceptable for consumption, whether it's cow, pig, goat, or camel. In fact, these aren't mentioned at all in 1 Corinthians. So this issue is not revolving around clean or unclean animals. Paul is writing to people he assumes understand the difference between what constitutes clean and unclean food. Rather, it's discussing the eating of animals that had been offered to pagan gods.

Paul says in 1 Corinthians 10:25, "Whatever is sold in the shambles," that's the meat market, "eat asking no questions." He was not telling buyers of meat to not ask, "Is this a cow or is this a pig?" That wouldn't make sense, because they could simply look at the carcass and quickly determine the animal.

The questions they weren't to ask: "Was this offered to a pagan god? What god was it offered to?"

He explains, "Don't ask those questions because once you know, then you're accountable." If they didn't know what pagan religious purposes these dead animals had fulfilled, then the issue would remain between the butchers and their false gods.

It's understood that the readers of Paul's letter would only be eating clean animals based on other Scripture in both the New and Old Testaments. That's why you don't find a reference to the kind of animal; that's not the issue since Paul already knows his readers will only eat clean meats.

The key then rests on verse 25, which says, "Without asking questions for conscience sake." That's where this makes most sense. Whether an animal is a pig or cow is a matter of content, not conscience. Conscience would only come into play with regard to the animal's purpose.

This is the context!

You'll find another indicator of this idea in Romans 14, where Paul says, "He that is weak eateth herbs." That doesn't mean vegetarians are weak! He's talking about those possessing a weak conscience being unable to eat anything sold in the shambles or the marketplace, because they are afraid that they might eat something that had been offered to a pagan god, even though they didn't participate in the practice.

So Paul basically says here, "Look, if you're really afraid that you might accidentally eat something someone else has offered to a god, even though you didn't offer it, and it's a clean animal, then just eat herbs." It's talking about a weak conscience, not a weak body.

Isn't Transfusing Blood the Same as Eating?

 Since the Bible says we should not eat blood, is it then wrong to receive blood transfusions?

A. Many people are surprised just to learn the simple fact that in the Old and New Testament, God's people—both of Jewish and Gentile—are clearly commanded not to eat blood (Genesis 9:4; Acts 15:29). This still applies to Christians today.

Knowing this, how should Christians handle the issue of blood transfusions? Some churches teach that a blood transfusion is no different than eating blood. I respectfully disagree, because I believe the admonition in the Bible is not to eat animal blood for food. (Of course, you shouldn't eat human blood for food either!)

This restriction of diet has both a spiritual and physical principle. Spiritually, the Bible says that the life is in the blood. And physically, we know that disease can be transferred from animal to animal by virtue of the blood.

When a person takes a blood transfusion, the purpose is to sustain that life. It's not for pleasure or to relieve hunger, and it isn't taken orally for nourishment. It's a completely different process—the blood type even has to match. In Acts 17:26, the Bible says that God has made all nations one blood. So the entire human family is related in that special sense. Indeed, we are all saved by virtue of a blood transfusion from Jesus.

I like to remind people that the first miracle of Christ was turning water into pure grape juice, and He gave it to celebrate a wedding. One of the last things Jesus did before He died on the cross was to taste sour wine. He gave us pure grape juice, and He took our offering of sour wine. It's symbolic of a lifesaving blood transfusion; that's what the blood of Christ does for us.

Common and Unclean?

 Q. Please explain Peter's vision of the sheet in Acts 10.

A. Some people try to use this passage to argue that God has done away with the distinction between clean and unclean meats. Anyone who uses the passage that way is either not reading the whole story or they're twisting the Scriptures to fit their own purposes, because the Bible is very clear.

The vision takes place approximately A.D. 34, about three-and-a-half years after Christ died. Peter says, "I have never eaten anything common or unclean." Obviously Peter had never heard Jesus condone eating unclean meats during His earthly ministry. Three times the sheet comes down, three times the voice says, "Rise, Peter; kill, and eat," and three times Peter says, "Not so, Lord; I have never eaten any thing that is common or unclean." Peter is left wondering what the vision meant. He knew it didn't mean to go against the clear Bible command not to eat the abominable animals.

While Peter is praying an interpretation of the vision, Gentile men approach him saying, "We want you to come and preach to the Gentiles." Peter later goes to the apostles and explains the vision himself: "God has shown me not to call any man"—that's M-A-N, not P-I-G, not clam, not vulture—"common or unclean." Peter went and preached to Cornelius and he, and his entire household, were baptized. Then the gospel began to go to the Gentiles. That was the reason for the vision. It had nothing to do with our digestion. It had to do with our attitude toward other groups of people that we think are unclean.

Why Do We Fast?

Q. What's the purpose of fasting?

A. There are several reasons why Christians might fast as part of their devotion to God. In the Bible, many of God's faithful turned to fasting to achieve varying and important ends to further His will. Many times, a person would fast for the purpose of repentance. For instance, when King David was exposed about his sin with Bathsheba, he fasted for seven days on his face (2 Samuel 12). In the New Testament, Paul fasted with no water or food for three days after it had been revealed to him that his killing of Christians was fighting against Jesus.

In addition, sometimes a person fasts for the purpose of pleading a special prayer before the Lord. In the book of Esther, all of God's people fasted for several days because they were seeking God's special attention. Jesus also said that when interceding for a soul captive to the devil, it might require a deeper level of prayer to have them delivered. "However, this kind does not go out except by prayer and fasting" (Matthew 17:21 NKJV).

A person might also fast because they want to better understand God's truth and seek the Lord's countenance. A great example of this is Daniel. His fast included not eating foods that were pleasant; he only ate very simple foods to keep his mind clear. In doing do, he would be better able to hear the voice and counsel of the Holy Spirit. Fasting also helps people control their appetites, which the Bible warns as dangerous. "And put a knife to thy throat, if thou be a man given to appetite" (Proverbs 23:2).

Fasting also has many health benefits. As the body's digestion rests, the mind seems to be more open to hear that "still small voice" (1 Kings 19:12). Of course, if someone struggles with low blood sugar, they may have more trouble with this—I encourage those with special medical conditions to seek the counsel of their doctor before fasting.

What's the Best Way to Fast?

 Is giving up all food and water the best way to fast?

A. Fasting is biblical, and I do believe it's important. But as a general rule, don't give up water. The only times people in the Bible went without water was for a severe fast involving life-or-death matters, and even then it was never for more than three days. Paul did such a fast, as did people in Esther's day.

There are many different ways of fasting. Daniel, for instance, fasted by eating no pleasant food. He ate very simple food for a period of time to keep his mind clear. I sometimes go on a V-8 Juice fast. It doesn't clog my system, yet it keeps my energy up so I can keep working. The idea is to clear your mind and present your body as a clean, living sacrifice before the Lord.

Paul's "Thorn in the Flesh?"

Q. What was Paul's "thorn in the flesh" mentioned in 2 Corinthians 12:7?

A. Most Bible scholars believe that Paul had a problem with his vision. There are a number of texts that support this theory in the New Testament. First, when he was converted, Paul—then Saul—went blind (Acts 9:8, 9). Then, in verse 18 it says that scales fell from his eyes and he could see. But it never says that he saw perfectly.

Paul had other people write his letters for him even though he was very brilliant, spoke many languages, and was very well educated. He only signed the letters himself. One time he said, "Ye see how large a letter I have written unto you with mine own hand" (Galatians 6:11). That didn't mean he'd written a long letter; it means big characters, because he couldn't see.

When Paul addressed the Sanhedrin in Acts 23, he denounced the high priest (verse 3). The people standing nearby said, "Revilest thou God's high priest?" (verse 4). Paul responded, "I wist not, brethren, that he was the high priest" (verse 5). He wasn't able to see that the one he addressed was the high priest, and he immediately apologized for his error.

In one of his letters Paul said, "If it had been possible, ye would have plucked out your own eyes, and have given them to me" (Galatians 4:15). People knew he had a problem with his eyes, so we believe the thorn in Paul's side was his vision.

It's similar to when Jacob wrestled with the angel when he was converted and limped the rest of his life after that experience. When Paul was converted, he temporarily went blind, but he still had sight problems the rest of his life.

Where Does Our Spirit Go After Death?

I understand that when we die, our physical bodies sleep until God raises us in our glorified immortal bodies. But what about our "spirit"? Where does it go after death?

The Bible tells us clearly in Ecclesiastes 12:7 that at death, "Then shall the dust return to the earth as it was: and the spirit shall return unto God who gave it." The spirit of life, the power of life, returns to God—but it's not conscious or awake. It is unable to reason or remember anything at all, because the Bible says, "For the living know that they shall die: but the dead know not any thing, neither have they any more a reward; for the memory of them is forgotten. Also their love, and their hatred, and their envy, is now perished; neither have they any more a portion for ever in any thing that is done under the sun" (Ecclesiastes 9:5, 6).

Jesus also describes Jarius's daughter in Luke as sleeping before He raises her from the dead. He also says this about Lazarus, who had been dead for four days. "Our friend Lazarus sleepeth; but I go, that I may awake him out of sleep" (John 11:11). Remember also that after Jesus raised Lazarus from the dead after the four days, Lazarus made no comment at all about his experience in death. He didn't know anything.

So it's a peaceful, dreamless sleep without consciousness of time. Of course, the next thing a believing person will be aware of is at the first resurrection with a new body. That's why Paul says, "Behold, I [show] you a mystery ... we shall all be changed, In a moment, in the twinkling of an eye, at the last trump" (1 Corinthians 15:51, 52). Adam died around 6,000 years ago, but he's going to come up with a new body instantly. Imagine that!

Can I Talk to the Dead?

 Can people really communicate with the dead?

The Bible clearly tells us in Isaiah 8:19 that we should not consult those who claim to be able to talk to the dead. The Law of Moses said that all who did so would be executed, because it's dabbling in diabolical spiritism. The person is actually communicating with demons, fallen angels, and not with some deceased loved one. Mortals do not have the power of resurrection, and even people inspired by the devil cannot communicate with the dead. The parable of the Rich Man and Lazarus tells us that there is a great gulf fixed between those two dimensions. And when humans try to talk to the dead, what they end up doing is talking with demons that are impersonating the dead. That's why it says in 2 Corinthians 11, "Even Satan himself is transformed into an angel of light." It is absolutely forbidden for Christians to even venture to talk to those who claim to talk to the dead. The Bible says that the living know they'll die, but the dead know not anything. That's Ecclesiastes 9:5. Job 34:14, 15 says, "His son has come to honor and he knows it not," speaking of a dead person. He doesn't know what's happening in his house and shall not return to it again. The dead don't know anything, and you can't talk to them until they're resurrected.

Are Near-Death Experiences Real?

 Does God allow people to have near-death experiences, and, if so, what is their purpose?

 A number of people have had so-called "near-death experiences." The most important thing to remember is that you should never build your understanding of Scripture based on a person's personal experience. Always base it on the Word of God. A doctor explained to me that what sometimes happens during extreme heart trauma is that the brain is robbed of oxygen. It's very dangerous when you don't get enough oxygen. Scuba divers know how easily this can happen. You can hallucinate and have visions. It's a biological occurrence. A person who claims to have risen out of their body or had a dream during near-death moments may have simply experienced a physiological phenomenon resulting from a lack of oxygen.

I wouldn't totally rule out the possibility that God is trying to speak to an individual personally through a vision. We've all had dreams where God communicates to us. But never build your theology on these dreams or near-death experiences, because they're all different and they often contradict each other.

Burial or Cremation?

 Does the Bible say anything about cremation?

A. I get this question periodically. However, I can't really give a direct answer from the Bible because there is no Bible mandate on how to bury someone. Typically in the Bible, people are buried when they die. It speaks of graves and how they are marked.

However, there are a few examples in the Bible of people who we know are saved who also happened to be cremated. You have Jonathan, the beloved friend of David, who was killed by the Philistines. His body was somewhat mutilated and then hung on a wall. (He was a type of Christ.) His body was rescued, or rather recovered, by the people of Jabesh Gilead. They burned the body, because it had been basically dismembered. And David blessed them, nor were they cursed, for doing that (1 Samuel 31:12).

In addition, the Bible says that we're ashes, that we came from ashes, and unto ashes we'll return. It's not a pretty subject, but we know that when a person dies and they're buried, they gradually decompose and they basically turn back into the elements of earth. That happens very slowly if we're put in a sealed coffin. But eventually, almost everything will rot unless you pay a lot of money to be cryogenically frozen. Or it can happen very quickly in a crematorium. But either way, we basically return to ashes.

Some people fear that if they're cremated, the Lord won't have enough body parts, like a bone, to piece them back together—that He won't be able to resurrect and reassemble them. But God is not going to use any of the old material. The Bible says, "All things are made new." He is going to take the essence of who we are, and put it in these new glorified bodies. So we don't need to worry if God can find the old parts.

But there's no command one way or the other, so we must assume that it was not a big issue with the Lord. Therefore, I ask people to let their conscience lead them.

Will My Loved Ones Know Me in Heaven?

 Will we recognize our loved ones in heaven?

 I sometimes like to start answering a question with asking another question. This is a perfect place to do so. When the saved get to heaven, will their perceptions and observations be better or worse, dull or enhanced? Obviously, it's going to be better.

The Lord says that "Now we see through a glass darkly, but then face to face. Now I know in part, but then shall I know even as I am known" (1 Corinthians 13). So our loved ones will know us, and we will know our loved ones. We won't have to walk around and take fingerprints in heaven to identify them, for we will have an enhanced knowledge.

What are the "Robes of Light"?

Some people say that when we're in heaven, we'll be wearing robes of light. Is this biblical?

The Bible does talk about angels that appear to be clothed with light, but nowhere in the Bible will you find the words "robes of light." Let's go back to Eden to get a clear picture of what it may be like for us in heaven.

There is a major misconception that Adam and Eve were streaking around the Garden of Eden—naked like a new-born baby! But in reality, Adam and Eve had garments of light that clothed them—an aura of light if you will—because they were righteous and they dwelled in the presence of God.

Here's another example: When Moses spent 40 days and 40 nights on the mountain talking to the Lord, he came down and was glowing. The Bible says he was shining so brilliantly that the people said, "Veil your face. We can't even look on you." So those who dwell in the presence of the holy God, those who are righteous, are surrounded by an aura of light.

Jesus said to the church, "You are the light of the world." I don't believe the Lord is going to have cotton robes, or linen robes, or wool or camel for robes in the kingdom. When Adam and Eve sinned, the light went out and then they were aware of their nakedness. They had no artificial clothing in the garden, that's why it says they were naked. But they weren't streaking around and suddenly realize it after eating the fruit. That would make it sound like the fruit actually made them smarter.

In the kingdom, when it talks about the saints who have these robes, we believe that these are living robes of light. It's based on what the angels wear. The Bible speaks of the angels of light. I don't think they've got weaving looms in heaven.

Modern Bible Translations—How Good are They?

Q. How good are the newer versions and translations of the Bible? Are there dangers in reading any of them?

A. Personally, I think that there are some dangers. Some of the new English versions are translated with a very strong bias. A friend of mine told me that his wife was looking at one of these "New Age" versions of the Bible. She wasn't very happy with it and said she wanted to go back to the "old age" version! I prefer versions that stay very close to "textus receptus." I've done a lot of research on it and heard arguments for and against new translations.

Let me explain a phenomenon. The King James Version of the Bible is public domain. So in order for publishers to make money by selling the Bible, they're required to say something different than existing versions in order to copyright, market, and own it. For instance, you can be sued for copying and quoting the New International Version without permission, because the publishers own that version. They have a monetary motivation to come up with something different, but how many ways can you say the same thing in English? I personally don't like the NIV very much. Paraphrases can be dangerous too. The Living Bible, for instance, isn't really a translation, it's a paraphrase—it's dangerous when you start calling the mark of the beast a tattoo.

The Lord can work through any version, and some of them are good for comparison. But when we start reading different versions of Scripture in church it starts to sound like Babylon. So my favorite versions for accuracy and symmetry are the King James and the New King James.

The Bible's First Author?

 Who was the first author of the Bible?

 The first writer in the Bible was Moses, but the first book Moses wrote was probably not Genesis. Most scholars believe that while Moses was a shepherd in Midian, taking care of sheep for his father-in-law, he probably wrote the book of Job. Then the second book he wrote was Genesis. As you probably know, the books in the Bible are not in a historical, chronological order. They're arranged in groups according history, poetry, and so forth.

First Published Bible?

 When was the Bible first published?

 The Bible was first published in the mid-15th century when Johann Gutenberg invented a new form of movable type that eventually led to the mass production of books. The Gutenberg Bible was printed in Mainz, Germany, around 1454 or 1455, and it was the first major book printed in the West. About 180 copies were printed, and significant parts of 48 copies still remain.

However, the Bible was preserved and duplicated for many centuries before Gutenberg published it. The books of the Old Testament existed before Jesus was born, and both He and His disciples called them "the law and the prophets" (Luke 16:16; John 1:45).

The Jews guarded the Old Testament Scriptures so carefully that if a scribe made a single mistake while making a copy, he had to destroy the entire manuscript! It was a life's work to make sure that every letter was just right, and curses were pronounced on any scribe who dared to alter God's Word in any way. This careful work paid off. The text of the Dead Sea Scrolls, which existed before the time of Christ, is almost exactly like the versions we have today.

After Jesus died, Mark, Matthew, Luke and John penned their Gospels and Paul wrote his letters. Many years later, godly men began to assemble all of the writings from the time of Christ, which they referred to as the New Testament. By A.D. 300, all of these books had been compiled to form the Bible that we still use today.

The Only Source of God's Truth?

Is the Bible the only source of God's truth, or can we trust inspired individuals?

The Bible is the foundation for all truth, but the idea that we cannot learn or God cannot speak through anything but the Bible is not biblical. If you look in 1 Corinthians 12–14, one of the gifts of the Spirit is prophecy. It's not a gift that ended with the Bible. God still speaks through people. But that doesn't mean we should measure the Bible by what they're saying. On the contrary, we must measure what prophets and pastors say by the Bible. The Bible is the criteria. It is unerring. We do not add to or take away from it. Isaiah says, "If they speak not according to this word, it is because there is no light in them" (Isaiah 8:20).

The Most Important Verse of the Bible?

 What is the most important verse in the Bible?

 I think if you ask 10 different people that question, you'll get at least 11 different answers! Martin Luther felt it was John 3:16, "For God so loved the world, that he have his only begotten Son, that whosoever believeth in him should not perish, but have everlasting life." He thought that encapsulated the gospel message. Many people believe it's one of the verses in Romans. "For the wages of sin is death; but the gift of God is eternal life through Jesus Christ our Lord" (Romans 6:23). One of my favorites is 2 Chronicles 7:14: "If my people, which are called by my name, shall humble themselves, and pray, and seek my face, and turn from their wicked ways; then will I hear from heaven, and will forgive their sin, and will heal their land." That's a wonderful verse! Another one of my favorites is Jeremiah 29:13, "And ye shall seek me, and find me, when ye shall search for me with all your heart."

What are the Two Horns of Revelation 13:11

What do the two horns in Revelation 13:11 represent? I keep hearing different things. Can you help?

A. That's a deep question. My answer assumes your familiarity with Revelation's symbols and their background.

The first beast arose out of the sea (Revelation 13:1). The four beasts of Daniel 7 also arose from the sea (verse 3). Since "sea" represents peoples and nations (see note on Revelation 13:1; 17:1, 2, 8), "earth" may reasonably be assumed to represent a sparsely settled region. The nation thus represented by the beast of Revelation 13:11 would therefore not arise by war, but would develop into greatness in a region of few inhabitants.

Commentators have seen in this second beast a symbol of the United States of America. This power accurately fulfills the specifications of the prophecy. As the first beast was going into captivity in 1798, the United States was growing in prominence and power. The nation arose not in the Old World, with its teeming multitudes, but in the New World, with its relatively few inhabitants.

The two horns may be taken to represent the two notable features of the American system of government, civil and religious liberty, both of which are guaranteed in its Constitution. Civil liberty found expression in a republican form of government and religious liberty in Protestantism.

Were There Two Sets of Cherubim in the Temple?

Q. In Exodus, the Bible says that the cherubim inside the most holy place of the tabernacle were on top of the ark, facing toward the center with their faces down and their wings over it. Later, when Solomon rebuilt the temple, he put in it a set of cherubim each with a wingspan of 5 cubits (2 Chronicles 3:11, 12). Were there two sets of cherubim in the temple when Solomon finished rebuilding it?

When the Lord instructed Moses to make the portable tabernacle, it was made as small and simple as possible for the purpose of transporting it through the desert and into Canaan. Then when Solomon made the permanent temple in Jerusalem, the cherubim in the Holy of Holies were made larger, with wings that stretched completely over the ark.

The Bible doesn't mention a second set of cherubim like the ones atop the Ark of the Covenant. However, angels were depicted throughout the entire temple—even woven into the veil (verse 14) and engraved in solid gold plating all around the walls (verse 7) and on the temple doors (1 Kings 6:31–35)—to represent the very real angels that continually surround God's heavenly throne.

The two angels that stand by the throne of God are the covering cherubs, and these special beings were symbolized in the earthly temple as the angels standing over the Ark of the Covenant. However, these two cherubim are by no means the only angels in heaven.

Daniel 7:10 tells about a thousand thousands ministering unto Him and 10,000 times 10,000 standing before Him. The prophet Daniel saw these ministering spirits surrounding the dwelling place of God. And in a different vision recorded in Isaiah 6, a prophet of God saw two creatures with six wings each standing by the throne of God. The golden cherubs in the temple were miniature models to help us picture the dwelling place of God in heaven.

The Least of His Worries

In Genesis 4:14, who is Cain worried will kill him?

This is the story where God pronounced a curse on Cain after he killed his brother Abel. "When you till the ground, it shall no longer yield its strength to you. A fugitive and vagabond you shall be on the earth" (Genesis 4:12 NKJV). He was driven away.

"Surely You have driven me out this day from the face of the ground; I shall be hidden from Your face; I shall be a fugitive and a vagabond on the earth, and it will happen that anyone who finds me will kill me" (verse 14 NKJV). Cain was saying that it was more than he could bear, and that people were going to hunt him down and kill him.

Adam, Eve, Cain, and Abel understood that they had been commanded to "Be fruitful, and multiply" (Genesis 1:22). Cain knew that in the process of time, people would procreate and there would be thousands of people in the world. Do you realize how many people could be born in the 900 years from that time until the Flood? It was likely hundreds of thousands of people.

Cain knew that he would be an outlaw—public enemy number one. He was anticipating that people would hunt him down and kill him as they multiplied and spread across the earth. Cain made that statement because he was anticipating what was going to happen as the earth became more populated.

The First Rainfall?

 When was the first rainfall? Was it during the time of Noah or before?

Genesis 2:6 says that before the Flood there had not yet been rain on earth. A "mist from the earth … watered the whole face of the ground." Perhaps it was God's own sprinkler system! Then it tells us that during the flood it rained for 40 days and 40 nights (Genesis 7:4). So the first rain as we know it came during the time of Noah. That's one reason no one had ever seen a rainbow until after the flood—up to that time there had been no rain!

Evil Spirits of the Lord?

 In 1 Samuel 16:14, the Bible talks about an evil spirit that came from the Lord. What does that mean?

Notice first that because Saul was no longer listening to the Lord (1 Samuel 15:26), God directed the prophet Samuel to anoint David as king in place of Saul. The Bible says that when Samuel poured the horn of holy oil on the young shepherd, "the spirit of the LORD came upon David from that day forward" (1 Samuel 16:13). Then in verse 14 it says that the Spirit of the Lord left Saul, "and an evil spirit from the LORD troubled him."

Set aside the phrase "from the LORD" for a second and focus instead on the part of the verse that says, "The spirit of the Lord departed from Saul." That would be the Holy Spirit, right?

The Holy Spirit came upon David and left Saul. When God's Spirit goes out of a person, the devil's spirit goes in. Jesus said in Matthew 12:30 that "He that is not with me is against me." Nobody is neutral. Everyone has varying degrees of either God's Spirit or the spirit of the enemy. To the same extent that we empty ourselves of self, God can fill us with His Spirit.

When the Bible says that "a spirit from the LORD" troubled Saul, it doesn't mean that God said, "I've got a devil I'm going to give to you." As evidence, look at the story of Job. When the devil came to the Lord and wanted to plague Job, he couldn't do anything until after God had withdrawn His protection from him. After God withdrew his protection from Job, He said, "He is in thine hand; but save his life," (Job 2:6). The next verse in the New King James Version goes on to say, "So Satan went out from the presence of the LORD, and struck Job with painful boils."

When the Bible says that an evil spirit came from the Lord, it means that God withdrew His protection from Saul after Saul rejected Him. When God withdrew His protection from Saul, these devils were allowed to bring a depression upon him.

The Bible says that "God … will not allow you to be tempted beyond what you are able, but with the temptation will also make the way of escape, that you may be able to bear it" (1 Corinthians 10:13 NKJV). This means that although God will allow you to be tempted, He's not doing the tempting. James 1:13 (NKJV) says, "Let no one say when he is tempted, 'I am tempted by God'; for God cannot be tempted by evil, nor does He Himself tempt anyone." God allows temptation to come in order to strengthen our characters, but He doesn't send it.

More Evil Spirits?

 Explain verses, like Isaiah 45:7, which say God sends evil to people.

You can also couple this verse with the verse that says, "The LORD sent an evil spirit to King Saul." And there's another place where Miciah the prophet is talking to Ahab and he said that he saw that the Lord sent a lying spirit to the prophets of Ahab. And then of course you have where it says that the Lord hardened Pharaoh's heart. In all of these verses it appears that evil is proceeding from God, yet the Bible says, "every good and perfect gift comes from God." If you read in the book of Job, you find the key that unlocks this relationship between good and evil and God's involvement. The devil is asking permission of God to tempt and torment Job. The devil cannot do anything without God allowing it. God must withdraw His protection, He must lift the hedge, and He must pull back His protective forces. And in that sense it appears that God is allowing the evil. The Lord is the one who placed the tree of the knowledge of good and evil in the Garden of Eden. That doesn't mean the Lord wants us to "eat" evil. It means that He gives us the freedom to choose. Sometimes the Lord withdraws His angels that protect us, and in that sense you could say that He is allowing evil to come. But James tells us that the Lord Himself does not tempt anyone, neither can He be tempted. The devil is an individual being, roaming about like a roaring lion, seeking whom he may devour. God is constantly putting him in check, to the degree of what He allows the devil to do. From time to time the Lord draws back his hand of protection to accomplish some purpose. This is why Paul says, "God is faithful, who will not allow you to be tempted beyond what you are able" (1 Corinthians 10:13). So when Isaiah says that evil comes from the Lord, it simply means that the devil can't do anything unless God allows it in His sovereign plan.

Doesn't Hell Burn Forever?

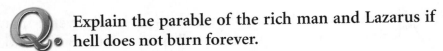

Explain the parable of the rich man and Lazarus if hell does not burn forever.

The story in Luke 16:19–31 is a parable. If we try to interpret this parable literally, we get into all kinds of trouble. First of all, it talks about the people in heaven and hell communicating. We already know that isn't biblical. If people in heaven are going to be communicating with people in torment through eternity, that's a very hideous, grotesque picture. Another thing is it talks about one drop of water cooling the tongue of a person who is in torment. That's obviously an exaggeration. Then finally it says that the beggar who dies and is saved goes to Abraham's bosom. There's no other Scripture anywhere that says that the saved go to the bosom of Abraham. If that's true, then he has one very large bosom! There's so much symbolic language in this story that if we take all the pictures literally, we're going to come up with a very distorted picture.

The lesson in the story of the rich man and Lazarus is often missed because people try to use it to prove their position on the state of the dead and hell. The lesson is that if God's people, who have the truth (the rich man), are not sharing their spiritual food with the lost (the beggar, Lazarus), that they may find that in the judgment that those they thought were lost will be saved and they themselves will be lost. In other words, we have a responsibility to share the gospel.

The message is the same for the church today. If we are building walls around our churches and saying that we're saved just because we're Christians, that we're going to study our Bibles together and forget about the lost of the world, then in the judgment we're going to find out that we didn't really love our brothers and we may be lost.

This parable has nothing to do with death and hell. Now suppose just for a minute that I start telling you a story that starts, "One day, Alice was walking in Wonderland." Immediately you know that I'm telling a fairy tale, parable, or allegory. As soon as Jesus used the word "hades" there, people knew he was going into a parable, because He obviously didn't believe in Greek mythological characters or places.

Sin in Heaven?

 Isaiah 65:20 seems to suggest that there will be sin in heaven. Is that true?

"There shall be no more thence an infant of days, nor an old man that hath not filled his days; for the child shall die an hundred years old; but the sinner being an hundred years old shall be accursed" (Isaiah 65:20). This text simply tells us that neither babies nor old people will die in heaven—death will be no more. The phrase "for the child shall die an hundred years old" tells us that time will be slowed down. Even at 100 years old, we will have just begun to live. Sin and sinners, on the other hand, will be no more. They shall "be accursed," which means that they will have been damned, not to return again.

Timeline of the Prophecies?

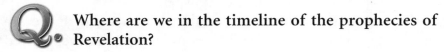

Where are we in the timeline of the prophecies of Revelation?

I believe we are living in the time described in Revelation 13 and 14. These chapters deal with the two great beasts. In chapter 13, the first beast is wounded and it recovers. This is a segment of time that has already passed. Then the second beast comes on the scene and is ready to make an image to the first beast that was healed.

According to Daniel 7, these beasts are nations. The second beast is the United States. It starts out looking like a lamb, but speaks like a dragon. In prophecy, a lamb is a symbol of Christ, and a dragon is a symbol of Satan. We are going to see America as a superpower, bringing the Protestant, Catholic, and Orthodox churches to apostatize—to abandon their distinctive beliefs and come together to form a one-world church. However, there will be a biblical element that will remain true. I also believe we are on the verge of religious laws that will hedge in God's people.